SUSAN ELKIN

Susan Elkin is an author and journalist, specialising in education and the performing arts. Education and Training Editor at *The Stage* since 2005 and a regular contributor for much longer, she also freelances for newspapers and magazines and has written over thirty books. Formerly a secondary English teacher for many years, Susan lives in Kent with her husband who is also her business manager. She is the mother of two grown-up sons.

Other titles in this series

SO YOU WANT TO BE AN ACTOR?
Prunella Scales and Timothy West

SO YOU WANT TO GO TO DRAMA SCHOOL?
Helen Freeman

SO YOU WANT TO BE A PLAYWRIGHT?
Tim Fountain

SO YOU WANT TO BE IN MUSICALS?
Ruthie Henshall with Daniel Bowling

SO YOU WANT TO DO A SOLO SHOW?
Gareth Armstrong

SO YOU WANT TO BE A THEATRE DIRECTOR?
Stephen Unwin

SO YOU WANT TO BE A THEATRE PRODUCER?
James Seabright

SO YOU WANT TO BE A TV PRESENTER?
Kathryn Wolfe

SO YOU WANT TO
WORK IN THEATRE?

Susan Elkin

NICK HERN BOOKS
London
www.nickhernbooks.co.uk

A Nick Hern Book

SO YOU WANT TO WORK IN THEATRE?
first published in Great Britain in 2013
by Nick Hern Books Limited
The Glasshouse, 49a Goldhawk Road, London W12 8QP

Cover designed by Peter Bennett
Typeset by Nick Hern Books, London

Printed and bound in Great Britain by
T.J. International, Padstow, Cornwall

A CIP catalogue record for this book
is available from the British Library

ISBN 978 1 84842 274 2

MIX
Paper from
responsible sources
FSC® C013056
FSC
www.fsc.org

To Rosie Elkin-Burr with my love.
Perhaps one day you'll want to work in theatre.

Contents

Introduction   1

Part One: First Steps   7

Part Two: Anything But Acting   29

    Creative   31

    Technical   63

    Administrative   97

    Other Jobs   113

Part Three: Acting – If You Really Must   145

Appendices

    Training in the UK   179

    Part-time class providers 182

Introduction

Theatre is like an iceberg. For every actor you see performing on stage, up to ten more people are behind the scenes, out of sight, working their socks off, one way or another, to bring the show to you.

> Theatre, without 'the' in front of it, is not a building. It means the whole activity of creating live performances and it can be done anywhere, in almost as many different ways as there are people. Think, for example, of the differences between street theatre, site-specific theatre, promenade theatre and devised theatre. Educator Rachel Kimber describes theatre simply and inclusively as 'the presentation of thoughts, concepts and emotions by individuals or groups to an audience', and I can't better that.

Some of these theatre workers, such as stage managers, dressers and scene-shifters, are physically close to the actors and only just out of the audience's sight. The people operating the lighting rig and sound system are slightly further away, but still nearby if this is theatre in a building.

Before the show you're watching saw the light of day, designers worked with the show's director. Then there are the people who made the costumes and built the sets to the designer's specifications. Together this creative team has ensured that the set, costumes, sound and lighting support the director's overall vision for the play – which had to be written by someone who may still be alive and around, if it's a modern piece.

Elsewhere in the venue, whatever form it takes, there may be a theatre manager and people selling tickets and programmes, collectively known as 'front of house'. Others could be on hand to sell you ice creams, interval drinks or other refreshments.

And behind the show is a producer or production company who invested money in it, or persuaded others to do so. Someone marketed the production so that the public knows about it. That means posters, flyers, internet exposure and working with the press.

It adds up to a large hidden workforce, all of it creative and skilled. There is a great deal more to 'working in theatre' than acting or performing, which is only the visible tip of that huge, unseen iceberg.

Really large companies, such as the Royal Opera House, National Theatre or Royal Shakespeare Company, employ hundreds of people, including some whose jobs you might not immediately associate with theatre. These include accountants, administrators, engineers, finance managers, health-and-safety staff, IT experts, human-resources managers, security staff, education managers, website developers, fundraisers – and more.

And once a show is finally staged, in comes the press, who write reviews so that their readers know what's on and whether or not it's any good. Theatre critics are, in a sense, 'working in theatre' too.

So is anyone else who writes about it. I, for instance, am working in theatre by writing for *The Stage* and by penning books like this one. And don't forget publishers such as Nick Hern Books either: everyone involved in the publication of this book is working in theatre too.

Opportunities

This book introduces you to some of these jobs and how you might get started in these many and various, exciting careers in theatre.

And the good news for young people wanting to work in theatre is that in many areas there is a serious shortage of people who can do many backstage jobs, especially the technical ones. The industry has – as everyone knows – plenty of actors, many of whom have to deal with long periods of unemployment. You are much more likely to find work backstage.

In 2008, research by the then newly founded National Skills Academy for Creative and Cultural Skills conducted a survey, which predicted that by 2017 the industry would be short of 30,000 skilled people to undertake backstage work for theatre and other live events. Some progress has been made since then towards setting up training opportunities to deal with this shortfall. That means more ways for you to get into these jobs.

The preparatory years

If you are serious about wanting to work in theatre, what should you be doing to prepare yourself? No one who wants to work in the industry can have too much theatre experience.

That is why the first section of this book is about grabbing every chance to 'do' theatre in the years before you start vocational training, which in many cases means while you are still at school, in your teens and/or even younger.

Choices

The second and longest section of this book is about the many different jobs in theatre that are open to you. You certainly don't have to act to work in theatre, although you probably need to be passionate about the world of theatre.

If, for instance, you love theatre but are good at, and drawn to, hairdressing, has it occurred to you that you might do hair and wigs in theatre?

Suppose a career as an electrician is beckoning, but you don't really want to turn your back on your beloved theatre. Why not combine the two and become a specialist live events or theatre lighting designer or technician?

Are figures and money what you're drawn to? Well, accountancy will probably please your parents and it will certainly pay the bills. But, if you're determined enough to work in theatre, you could aim for an accountancy job within the performing-arts industry. Or you might consider producing, which is all about money.

The options and combinations are almost endless.

And if you really must...

Finally, of course, although I've been playing down performance as a way of working in theatre, every show needs a cast. Even though, as we've seen, they are just the visible tip of the iceberg, theatre also depends on its frontmen and women – its actors.

That's why the last section of this book tells you about some of the routes open to you if you are determined to act, and how you might fund training.

It also discusses some of the less obvious professional jobs actors might consider, such as corporate acting or working in schools as facilitators.

One of this book's main messages, however, is that there are many more lucrative and reliable opportunities to work in theatre off the stage than on it.

Part One

First Steps

You may have caught the theatre bug long ago. Maybe you've been to the theatre and seen a few shows – perhaps pantomime, plays for children, performances of your school examination texts, or just theatre for fun – and wondered what you have to do to get professionally involved.

Then someone tells you that actors – and many backstage workers – train in drama schools. These are specialist colleges, often attached to universities, providing vocational training for people who want to work in theatre. Very few people succeed in technical or performance roles in this industry without that training.

Well, you won't be taken seriously by a drama school if you turn up at an audition or interview without having had any practical experience. Seeing shows produced and performed by others is not enough, although it's important to see as much theatre as you can.

So, if you're serious, you need to search out and seize as many opportunities as you can to work, or at least be active, in theatre long before you consider vocational training in any aspect of the performing-arts industries.

Apart from anything else, it will give you some sense of what working in theatre is really like and how productions are created. You may, when you've tried it, decide that it isn't what you want to do after all – and it's much better to find that out before you embark on expensive, time-consuming vocational training if you realise that this isn't the right area of work for you.

So how are you going to build up your experience?

Local part-time classes

There are many teachers and schools offering weekend or evening classes in acting, singing and dancing for children and teenagers, often as an extra-curricular activity in addition to their primary- or secondary-school education elsewhere. A 'triple threat' package which gives you a taste of all three is quite common.

Backstage skills are less frequently taught this way. But since there are always shows being put on, it's worth asking if, instead of performing, you can help with stage management, sound or lighting if that's where your interest lies.

You must first choose between the local branch of an established (or new) chain of a branded, franchised company, or an independent, stand-alone part-time school.

There are pros and cons either way, of course. A big-name franchise comes with an established, recognisable 'brand' and a way of working that is controlled by head office. On the other hand, an independent school is often cheaper and more flexible.

You may have an excellent local, independently run school which enjoys a good reputation. If you are new to all of this, do your homework and talk to other young people who attend them, and to their parents.

Make sure that the school you are considering has some sort of accreditation – the National Council for Dance Training's minimum standards badge, if the school is teaching dance, for instance – so that you know the quality is up to scratch.

Check too that the teachers are properly qualified and have DBS clearance (DBS is the Disclosure and Barring Service, merging what was previously the Criminal Records Bureau (CRB) and the Independent Safeguarding Agency (ISA) checks). Ensure that the premises are maintained to a decent standard. You may find that an independent school charges less than a franchised school (no head-office over-heads), which is a bonus if you can find a good one.

On the other hand, perhaps you favour the equivalent of Waitrose or Tesco over a small, independent food shop, and feel happier with a branded name and a larger umbrella organisation. In that case, names such as Razzamataz, Stage-coach or the Pauline Quirke Academy are for you.

Try the public library, a business directory or use the inter-net to find out which franchise groups operate in your area. Unless you are in a very densely populated and extensive urban area, your choice is likely to be constrained by which franchises have schools nearby.

The advantage of a franchised school is that you know exactly what you are getting, because the curriculum is usu-ally designed centrally and is common to all its branches. That means teachers work to specific lesson plans and term themes or topics. This is useful too if your family moves to another part of the country because, if you can find a school in the same group, you can start seamlessly from where you left off.

The common curriculum also means that franchised schools can work together in regional or national projects, which provide participating pupils with extra performance and development opportunities alongside the ones they get in their own local school – one of Theatretrain's great strengths, for instance.

You can research any franchised chain, of course, by looking at the company's website to find out about its ethos, way of working, group sizes, age range, charges and so on (see Appendices).

Remember that no two are exactly the same and that each has its unique selling points, so it's worth looking at carefully. Music Bugs (classes for age six months to four years), The Courage to Sing (tuition for adults) and Soundsteps (keyboard/piano lessons in over 100 centres), for instance, specialise in music rather than in dance or drama. Others, such as New Youth Theatre, tend to be more drama dominated.

Then, if you find one you like the look of, you can search to see whether there's a school a convenient distance from where you are. You can find a list of some chains of part-time class providers in the Appendices at the back of this book.

Local youth theatre

Youth theatres are essentially clubs dedicated to developing and presenting shows with young people. Within a good youth theatre, there is usually scope for young people to get involved with every aspect of the production, including all backstage jobs, front of house and marketing.

Some youth theatres are based in venues and led by adults who work in the venue in other capacities, often directing.

For example, there's a youth theatre company with about sixty members aged nine to eighteen at Helmsley Arts Centre in Ryedale, Yorkshire which meets weekly in term time to take part in workshops, to rehearse for productions, or to devise projects.

Members are encouraged to develop their acting skills and to learn about the technical and backstage aspects of theatre. It costs £28 per term at the time of writing – which makes it far cheaper than any part-time class.

Recently, several members successfully auditioned for the National Youth Theatre and were cast in productions at venues such as York Theatre Royal and West Yorkshire Playhouse. Some have gone on to drama school in London or to university to study theatre.

Or take the youth theatre run by Dorset School of Acting, which is based in the Lighthouse at Poole. It runs sessions for everyone aged from three to twenty-one and gives them lots of training and opportunities to perform or to support performance.

These are just two examples picked at random from the many similar youth theatres all over the country. Contact your local theatre and ask if it has a youth theatre you can join.

Youth theatres are also sometimes run by secondary and primary schools as an adjunct to the curriculum or as some sort of after-school club. Sometimes a drama teacher will lead a youth theatre in his or her own school at weekends – and typically it would be open to all young people, not just the ones who attend that school.

National opportunities in youth theatre

In addition to taking part in your local youth theatre, once you have some experience, and if you're still keen, you might consider applying to one of the organisations which offer youth theatre nationally.

National Youth Theatre

The most famous of these is the National Youth Theatre. Every summer it brings together some of the most theatrically talented teenagers in Britain to engage in classes and workshops and to create a show during a two-week course.

Some of its members are actors, others are passionate about backstage work and technical theatre – they have all undergone a rigorous selection process.

Founded in 1956 by Michael Croft, a south London secondary-school teacher of English and drama, NYT's first ever production was *Henry V*. Since then it has helped to train performers such as Helen Mirren, Derek Jacobi, Matt

Lucas, Romola Garai, Jamie Theakston and many more who have gone on to glittering professional careers.

Students who audition successfully for NYT are enrolled on one of the two summer courses – one for over-eighteens and the other for under-eighteens. These courses, on which places are limited, are very intensive and lead to an end-of-course performance which is not open to the public. Those who complete the course satisfactorily are invited to become NYT members.

Members also get the chance to take part in productions on the West End stage and in major venues around the UK and abroad. In recent years, opportunities have included performing in Beijing at the 2008 handover ceremony to the London 2012 Olympics, in Abu Dhabi at the 2009 FIFA Club World Cup, and in Shanghai at World Expo 2010.

In 2012, NYT members took part in the London 2012 Olympic and Paralympic's Team Welcome Ceremonies, a bilingual adaptation of a Shakespeare classic and a filmed documentary drama about the 1948 Olympics – among many other projects.

NYT, which reaches twenty thousand young people every year, also runs free courses and workshops for non-members. *Talking to Byron*, for instance, was a show about knife crime devised and performed by 'creative assistants' who toured schools in and around London with their work, supported by the Home Office. It ran a similar project in Birmingham, with support from the Equalities and Human Rights Commission.

Based in offices in Southwark, near Tower Bridge, and with large rehearsal rooms on Holloway Road in North London, NYT runs its courses and activities all over Britain – with a strong network of regional groups – in order to be as inclusive as possible, although the core of its work continues to be showcasing the theatrical abilities of exceptionally talented youngsters. So it is not easy to get in.

Youth Music Theatre UK

Another youth theatre operating nationally is Youth Music Theatre UK (www.youthmusictheatreuk.org), which was founded in 2003. It is one of the National Youth Music organisations supported by Youth Music.

YMTUK runs one-week summer schools for eleven- to twenty-one-year-olds in the South East and near Edinburgh, where it has an office in addition to its main office in London. It also offers training opportunities for recent graduates and emerging artists.

Jon Bromwich is the YMTUK's Executive Producer.

'We work almost exclusively with new work, either by commissioning new musical theatre from experienced writers and composers, or through the devising process. To this end we employ active industry professionals at the top of their game. Creativity is at the heart of the work and we actively encourage as much participation as we can from the young people who join the company.

Most, although not all, of our work is residential. So we have a substantial duty of care to the seven hundred young people who stay with us on our courses during each year.

We seek to make the company open to a wide range of young people from different backgrounds, and try to promote outreach and local projects as much as possible, and to provide hardship funds and bursaries to help those who cannot afford the courses.'

Royal Opera House Youth Company

In 2010, the Royal Opera House launched its first Youth Opera Company. It made its debut in May that year in a specially commissioned new work called *Beginners* by composer Richard Taylor and librettist Jane Buckler. There was also a newly devised piece that included a number of opera choruses written for young voices.

Work continued with the Youth Company providing the children's chorus for *La bohème* in the opera house in Covent Garden in 2012.

The idea is to offer young people from a wide variety of backgrounds and who possess untapped potential, the opportunity to discover and develop their talent. The company's fifty or so members, aged nine to twelve, are drawn from across London and the South East.

So how are the participants selected? An initial group of more than four hundred schoolchildren took part in an extensive series of participatory workshops. Ongoing recruitment workshops find a small number of new members to filter in each year. The aim is to keep the recruitment base as broad as possible and to provide opportunities for everyone, irrespective of whether or not they have previous experience of opera.

Summer schools

Short courses, like the ones by YMTUK, run during school holidays, and can be a good way of giving you an immersive, perhaps life-changing experience.

There is also plenty of potential in summer schools and other holiday courses for adults, including professional theatre technicians and actors. We will look at some of these in Parts Two and Three. For the moment, let's concentrate on opportunities for young people who are still investigating options before making long-term career decisions.

Almost every drama and stage school now offers a range of summer schools at different levels. And many other organisations, such as performing-arts venues and music-teaching schools and companies run them too. Some have quite a general focus, while others are very specific.

The Egg, for example, is Theatre Royal Bath's award-winning theatre for children, young people and their families. Its annual summer school usually has places for sixty young people aged twelve to twenty-one, with opportunities for backstage work as well as performing.

The highly esteemed Sylvia Young Theatre School runs popular, good-quality holiday courses in its new building off Edgware Road in London. These weeks are for ages ten to eighteen, although the students are grouped according to age. Sylvia Young usually also offers a theatre-skills course for ages eight to eighteen. It includes drama/audition technique, singing and microphone technique, street dance and basic circus skills.

'While I was still at school, I did a one-week summer school at East 15 Acting School in Essex and it changed my life. I discovered that there are such wonderful things as voice and movement classes and decided, then and there, that I never wanted to study anything academic ever again. So I applied for the full-time course.'

Stuart Walker, East 15-trained actor

Bristol Old Vic Theatre School offers a theatre-skills week for children aged approximately seven to fifteen in two groups. Like most summer schools, it leads to an end-of-course performance.

Respected specialist vocational drama school Guildford School of Acting has long experience in summer-school provision. In a typical year, it might offer a six-day GSA Juniors course for ages eight to eleven, a musical-theatre week for fifteen- and sixteen-year-olds, and a youth-theatre course for twelve- to fourteen-year-olds. All GSA's summer courses take place in the school's new building on the University of Surrey campus, just down the hill from Guildford Cathedral.

As well as running weekly classes, most of Stagecoach Theatre Arts's six hundred centres run summer-holiday workshop weeks which are open to those aged eight to eighteen (and not limited to Stagecoach regular class attenders). There are also some options for younger children in some places.

The Royal Conservatoire of Scotland (formerly the Royal Scottish Academy of Music and Drama) is in Glasgow. It offers a good range of imaginative summer courses for children and teenagers. A typical year might include work on a specific show or theme for ages five to seven, and musical theatre for ages fifteen to seventeen.

The Theatre Royal Bury St Edmunds is a well-known and respected producing and receiving venue. It is also busy on the community and education front, running an annual summer school for those aged thirteen to twenty-one. Auditions are usually held in April.

There are, literally, hundreds of opportunities like these all over the country every summer, and sometimes during Easter or Christmas holidays too. The small selection I've mentioned here is just to give some idea of the range available. For more options, look at www.summer-schools. info/performing-arts.

Grabbing opportunities

At school

Unless you are very unlucky, your everyday school will be putting on an occasional show, the school play – make sure you are involved. It might be a pretty basic show directed by a well-meaning teacher, or you might be lucky enough to be in a school with a professional theatre and very experienced drama and technical staff to lead the work in it.

Some schools employ a professional director-in-residence to work with students on a specific production. Others have schemes to bring in an actor-in-residence or a theatre technician-in-residence. These are all people from whom you can learn a great deal. Unlike many schoolteachers – who have different skills – these are people with recent, relevant industry experience.

Remember that 'working in theatre' at school doesn't mean acting and nothing else. You can help backstage; you can work on the lighting or the sound; you might design the set, costumes, programmes or even tickets. Someone has to show people to their seats, sell programmes, serve refreshments and many other jobs too. Or, if it's a musical and you're a musician, you might find yourself playing in the band.

You can also learn a lot through drama course options in secondary schools including GCSE Drama, A level Theatre Studies or Highers in Scotland. Many schools offer BTEC Firsts (roughly equivalent to GCSE) and BTEC Nationals (roughly equivalent to A level) in a range of performing-arts subjects. BTECs tend to be very hands-on and practical.

Amateur theatre

In almost every area, there is a drama, operatic or musical-theatre group rehearsing and presenting shows for the love of it, in the evenings and at weekends. Some are pretty humble efforts, others achieve near professional standards.

Although these are clubs usually joined by adults, most are delighted to have younger members.

You may need to be sixteen to join because of child-protection issues – you cannot expect every member of the group to pay for a DBS check in order to work with one or two under-sixteens in the company. One way around this is for a young member to have a designated adult – or chaperone – who agrees to be responsible for him or her. In practice, many young people join amateur groups because their parents or other relatives are members, and that solves the problem. Such groups can provide all the same sorts of learning experiences as school productions.

The National Operatic and Dramatic Association (NODA) is the linking body for amateur theatre. It gives 'professional support for amateur theatre', and provides the sector with a collective voice. It has members all over Britain. It also runs summer schools to help amateur-theatre enthusiasts to hone their skills in a range of theatre-related disciplines.

Seeing theatre and volunteering

If you want to work in theatre, then you can't see too much of it. You need to see as many shows as you can and keep your diet as varied as possible.

See Shakespeare and other classic plays. Watch as much new work as you can, including devised pieces and site-specific theatre. Keep an eye open for interesting companies which produce innovative work and might be touring in your area. Look out for Propeller, Hull Truck, Shared Experience and Pilot, among many others.

Don't forget theatre for young audiences, as it employs many people who work in theatre these days. Companies such as Oily Cart, M6 and Kneehigh are producing breath-taking work. Musicals are always popular, so musical theatre is where a lot of the work is – include this in your diet too.

Theatregoing is, of course, expensive, but many theatres and other venues have deals and special offers for students and young people.

Alternatively, you could try volunteering, or seeking part-time paid work, at your local theatre. Cambridge Arts Theatre, Stratford East or the Marlowe Canterbury have ongoing programmes of touring theatre which visits for a short run – these are known in theatre jargon as receiving theatres. If you can persuade the theatre to let you work as an usher or programme-seller – or even loading the dishwasher in the café or cleaning the loos – you will probably be given tickets for shows which haven't sold out, or at least be able to slip in for the second half.

In this way, you can learn a lot about how the business of theatre works – very useful for someone who wants to work in theatre.

Getting careers advice

Sadly, it can be difficult for young people to find out what they need to know about working in theatre. Because actors and other performers are the most visible and obvious workers in a theatre, few people – and that includes some teachers and careers advisers – know much about the other theatre jobs available.

This is why so many students, and their anxious parents, are told that actors spend most of their time 'resting' – i.e. out of work – and that 'a nice career in law, with a bit of amateur theatre on the side if you must' would be more sensible.

It is true that, although the performing-arts industries continue to grow despite recessions, credit crunches, economic downturns or whatever term you use, Britain trains more actors than it has jobs for.

For any role in theatre, there has to be a number of actors for a casting director to choose from. Think how low standards would be if we were short of actors and there were only one or two possibilities for each job, thereby leaving the casting director obliged to take what she or he could get.

On the other hand, let's not forget that the picture is not all gloom. There are plenty of *other* jobs in theatre – as we shall see, in detail, in Part Two of this book.

Too many students are badly advised, because many schools want as many students as possible to go to university – and they tend to sway parents.

Paul Durose is Theatre Manager and Senior Technician at The Leys School in Cambridge. He is also the co-founder of the Schools Theatre Support Group – an organisation for professional theatre staff working in education – which also helps to promote theatre careers and encourage the next generation of theatre workers.

'When I set about getting into a career behind the scenes, I found there was very little help or support available from any quarter: careers advisers, school, press, parents. My career really came about as an accident of sorts. Through most of secondary school, I was determined to become an architect or town planner. However, as things turned out, A levels weren't for me, so I found myself having to search for a new career path. Whilst sitting behind a lighting console at the amateur theatre where I spent most of my free time (possibly the cause of my lack of commitment to A levels), I had one of those moments of revelation when suddenly things click into place. I remember thinking, "What do I enjoy which I can do for a job?" I looked down at the console and suddenly thought: "Somebody must do this for a career."

Turning my revelation into a training path and long-term career was more difficult. The school careers department didn't have a clue. Neither did the Job Centre. Nor did I know where to look for jobs or where to find more training. My parents were supportive, but only because they also were theatrically inclined, so knew there was potentially a viable career to be had. Eventually I found a BTEC course, which led to a university degree course, and on into work.

I now work in a school managing the theatre, supporting the drama department and running the shows. I also run an activity club for keen students who want to help out backstage – as I did when I was at school myself. We have a reasonable list of past students working in the industry – ranging from film producers to company directors to lighting designers – but there is still a lack of awareness that backstage careers exist. Students can be put off following an active interest and talent. There is pressure to "do well", pressure from parents to strive for a "normal" career, and a lack of awareness in schools' careers departments.

I searched recently and found the drama prospectuses hidden away on the bottom shelf in the careers library – and even then, only one or two had any technical or design-related courses.'

If you really want to do technical theatre or acting, a university drama course may not be the best option. It might *not* give you the level of practical work or the teaching hours you need to be industry-ready. And once you've done it, you will have used up your eligibility for student-loan funding. If you decide to retrain in a drama school at that stage, it may be prohibitively expensive.

If you want a more academic course – perhaps with a view to becoming a theatre critic or playwright – then, of course, a university course could well be the way forward. But for practical skills, sometimes it is not.

So how are you going to find out about those other careers in theatre?

Creative Choices

Creative and Cultural Skills is part of the government's National Skills Academy. Each autumn it organises a series of events called Creative Choices (formerly Offstage Choices). From small beginnings in 2009, there are now over a hundred of these each year and the project continues to grow.

CCS works with twenty 'founder' further-education colleges, each of which presents a day in a local performing-arts venue for thirteen- to fifteen-year-olds. The professionals who work in the venue talk to the visitors about their work and, in many cases, give them opportunities to have a go. I watched a group of students stage-manage a scenery change on the *Grease* set at the Piccadilly Theatre in the West End, for instance.

'I'm learning so much here today,' Ryan, a fourteen-year-old student from Phoenix High School in West London, said halfway through an event at the Lyric Hammersmith. Ryan and his classmates, along with a group from Fulham Cross Girls' School, learned about communications, development activities, visitor-management and directing from people who do these jobs at the Lyric. 'I'd no idea there was so much to it,' observed a girl studying GCSE Drama.

In the afternoon, the students were introduced to the nitty-gritty of staging a show. Chris Harris, Head of Lighting at the Lyric, and Nick Manning, Head of Sound, showed them some tricks and techniques. All the students tried making some elementary set-design decisions under the guidance of freelance designer Marise Rose.

The intensive day ended with a question-and-answer session, with a panel energetically chaired by Rachel Tyson, the Lyric's Young People's Producer. The line-up included Sarah-Jane Chapman, Deputy Head of Development and Communications at LAMDA (who was there to answer questions about drama school), several students, and a number of practitioners.

No two Creative Choices events are the same because each is run by a venue in partnership with a college. And there is no definitive way of doing it.

'It was a marvellous example of a theatre building on the lessons of the previous year and a great template for any venue seeking to get involved with the scheme. It combined two essential elements – giving youngsters a chance not only to hear and observe, but to take a hands-on role, and showing them how an offstage contribution plays a vital role in the finished production.'

Brian Attwood, Editor of The Stage, *after attending Creative Choices at Luton Hat Factory.*

High House Production Park

Near the Dartford Crossing in Thurrock is the Royal Opera House's magnificent new production centre. Here, all scenic construction for its shows takes place and there are vocational training opportunities which we will come to in Part Two.

ROH's entire education department is now based nearby on the same very attractive site – in a Grade Two-listed building – next to NSA Creative and Cultural Skills's new building.

It organises many projects to help school and older students learn. For example, in 2012 it ran a competition for composers aged eleven to sixteen. Competitors were invited to compose a fanfare.

Also in 2012 there was a project relating to *La bohème*. Students attending NSA Creative and Cultural Skills's founder colleges were invited to test and develop marketing and production skills. They got feedback from senior ROH staff and some of their work was exhibited in the Covent Garden building during the run of the production.

Teachers and students should check the ROH website and contact the education department for more information about current learning opportunities.

TheatreCraft

TheatreCraft is an annual careers fair for young people aged seventeen to twenty-five, organised by Masterclass, Theatre Royal Haymarket's education arm, in partnership with Royal Opera House where the event is held in late autumn.

'I'm so glad I brought my thirteen students here today. It's such a wonderful opportunity for them to get into the heart of theatreland and to find out about so many performing-arts jobs from so many expert practitioners.'

Orwain Rose, drama teacher at Haringey Sixth Form College.

Drama schools and other organisations such as IdeasTap and the London College of Fashion are also there with stands to give information about jobs and training to students.

Elsewhere in the building, over a thousand young people learn through the day in seminars led by people such as Rob Young, LAMDA's Head of Technical Theatre, and Mark Shenton of *The Stage*, about the many 'behind the scenes' facets of the performing-arts industry and the available careers opportunities – from lighting to theatre journalism, from wig-making to marketing or designing.

Open Doors

The Royal Shakespeare Company runs an annual careers event in Stratford-upon-Avon, for young adults aged over sixteen.

Participants take part in workshops run by various back-stage departments at the RSC – stage management, lighting, sound, automation and more.

It's an opportunity to learn about the variety of backstage careers available, and the skills and qualifications that are required to begin a career behind the scenes in theatre. The event usually runs early in the year.

The National Student Drama Festival

The National Student Drama Festival (NSDF), held each spring usually in Scarborough, is another training opportunity. Groups (aged sixteen and over) from schools, universities, colleges, youth theatres and so on, present their shows and attend workshops during a very intense festival week.

> Talk to the people who run your local youth theatre, classes or venue about careers in theatre. They have hands-on experience and are more likely to give you the wide-ranging, disinterested, open-minded advice and information you need.

Further reading

The Methuen Drama Dictionary of the Theatre, ed. Jonathan Law (Methuen Drama, 2011)

Oxford Companion to Theatre and Performance, ed. Dennis Kennedy (Oxford, 2010)

Contacts: The Essential Book of Contacts for the Entertainment Industry, published annually by Spotlight, 7 Leicester Place, London WC2H 7RH. www.contactshandbook.com, sales@spotlight.com, 020 7440 5056. It is also sold in bookshops such as Waterstones.

The Stage, published weekly on Thursdays, carries a great deal of information about achieving industry readiness and preparing for it. Specific aspects – such as franchised schools, summer schools, part-time training and so on across the whole range of work in theatre – are covered in up-to-date detail in annual supplements. See the website for even more.

Never underestimate the power of fiction as a source of information. Lyn Gardner is a well-known theatre critic, and her series of books for children and young adults about Olivia (published by Nosy Crow) is set in a stage school – quite an insight.

Useful websites

Bristol Old Vic Theatre School (summer school)
www.oldvic.ac.uk/get-skilled-up

Creative Choices www.nsa-ccskills.co.uk/offstage-choices

Dorset School of Acting www.dorsetschoolofacting.co.uk

The Egg www.theatreroyal.org.uk/the-egg

Guildford School of Acting (summer school)
www.gsauk.org/summer-school.php

Helmsley Arts Centre
www.helmsleyarts.co.uk/youth+theatre

High House Production Park
www.highhouseproductionpark.co.uk

Masterclass www.masterclass.org.uk

National Student Drama Festival www.nsdf.org.uk

National Youth Theatre www.nyt.org.uk

National Operatic and Dramatic Association
www.noda.org.uk

Royal Shakespeare Company (careers event)
www.rsc.org.uk/about-us/work/open-doors.aspx

Schools Theatre Support Group www.stsg.org.uk

The Stage www.thestage.co.uk

Stagecoach www.stagecoach.co.uk

Sylvia Young Theatre School
www.sylviayoungtheatreschool.co.uk

Summer Schools
www.summer-schools.info/performing-arts

Theatre Royal Bury St Edmunds www.theatreroyal.org

TheatreCraft www.theatrecraft.org

Youth Music Theatre UK www.youthmusictheatreuk.org

Part Two

Anything But Acting

I have divided the non-performance jobs in theatre into the following categories as a convenient way of organising the material in this section.

- CREATIVE
- TECHNICAL
- ADMINISTRATIVE
- OTHER

And if you want more information or you're interested in something I haven't covered in this book, then try www.getintotheatre.org, which gives very detailed accounts of various jobs.

CREATIVE JOBS

So who are all those people whose creative work and ideas lie behind the performance you see on stage, and what do you have to do to join them?

- DIRECTOR   32
- CASTING DIRECTOR   38
- MUSICAL DIRECTOR   42
- OTHER DIRECTORS   44
- PLAYWRIGHT   46
- DESIGNER   52

Director

What does a director do?

The director is the person who leads the actors and other performers as they interpret the text to be performed.

He or she has a creative vision and gives instructions – or makes suggestions – to bring those ideas to life on stage. The director leads rehearsals and liaises with everyone involved in the production.

Traditionally, theatre directors were quite dictatorial people. They arrived at rehearsals with firm ideas and told the cast what they wanted done.

Today, rehearsing is often a much more collaborative process in which director and cast – with the playwright if it's a new piece – will try out various ideas and then make decisions about what works best.

The director, however, is clearly in charge and will have the last word. And no two directors will operate in exactly the same way. Some, even now, will be more assertive in their demands than others.

When the rehearsal period ends and the show opens, the director will sit in the audience on the first night – and then usually step away from the production. Most directors are freelance and quite often he or she moves on immediately to begin rehearsing another show with another company.

There may be occasional 'visits', however, when the director makes observations and gives performers 'notes' about how the minutiae of the show could be improved.

A large company also often has assistant directors, directorial assistants, interns, trainees or others who take some of the rehearsals and help oversee the show as it beds down.

How do you become a director?

Many directors have been actors first. Gregory Doran, Artistic Director of the Royal Shakespeare Company, for example – with dozens of highly acclaimed shows under his belt – initially joined the RSC as an actor in the 1980s.

Similarly, Daniel Evans, Artistic Director of Sheffield's Crucible Theatre, was a successful actor (trained at Guildhall School of Music and Drama) who turned to directing. Michael Grandage, former Artistic Director at the Donmar Warehouse and now running his own company, was an actor before he was a director too.

Some people decide that they don't have it in them to act, but definitely want to work in theatre as directors.

Katie Mitchell is an Associate Director at the National Theatre, where her work has included *Women of Troy, The Seagull, Ivanov, Iphigenia at Aulis* and *Three Sisters*. She has also worked for the RSC, the Royal Court and extensively in opera. Her highly successful career takes her all over Europe.

She did a lot of drama at boarding school (Godolphin, Salisbury, and Oakham, Rutland), but soon realised that she was not a good actor.

Deciding at the age of sixteen that she wanted to be a director, she took her own company to the Edinburgh Fringe. After gaining an English degree at Oxford, Mitchell's first professional job was in stage management and typing scripts at the King's Head Theatre in Islington.

Always determined and focused, she worked as an assistant at Paines Plough and at the RSC. Then came her big, life-changing experience when, in 1989, she won a bursary from the Winston Churchill Trust to study directing in Russia, Georgia, Poland and Lithuania, with many of the great and famous practitioners – just after the collapse of the Soviet Bloc.

Mitchell believes that directing is very hard to do well because a good director needs so many skills. 'You need to be both a visual and an aural thinker so that you can work with the look and sound of something. You also need to be able to paint a scene with light and to be accomplished at analysis,' she says. 'Then there's psychology. You have to be able both to manage the psychology of the group you're working with and to help them to understand the psychology of the characters they're playing.'

She continues: 'It's a very difficult, bespoke craft – perhaps like cabinet-making – and it takes a very long time to learn.' Not that she believes she has it 'right' even now. She says several times during our conversation that she is still learning from 'a lifetime of failed productions'.

University is probably a good training ground – rather than drama school if you don't intend to act first – because a degree in English Literature or Drama will give the opportunity to do plenty of in-depth textual analysis.

Although English might be a good choice, some practitioners believe that it doesn't really matter what subject an aspirant director does at university. Just learn about something and do as much drama as you can while you're there, they argue, conceding that if you opt for Theatre Studies or Drama it might maximise the opportunities for student productions.

While at university, try and get to the Edinburgh Fringe with a show you are directing and mix with as many professionals as you can. Contacts are important and only you can build them.

After university, look for a company in which you can work as some sort of assistant to the director. Think of it as part of your training and be prepared – unless you get a very lucky break – to do it for little or no pay to begin with.

Start a small company of your own. Create and direct work and get it seen. You learn to direct by directing, and the most important thing is to get as much experience as you can.

If, after you've completed a BA degree, you want specific training in directing, there are a number of one-year, postgraduate diplomas or MA training offered by reputable colleges and other organisations.

East 15 Acting School (part of the University of Essex), Royal Central School of Speech and Drama (University of London), Royal Holloway (University of London) and Royal Academy of Dramatic Art (RADA), for example, offer postgraduate directing courses – and that is only a random handful. There are many more possibilities.

But be aware that almost all postgraduate training has to be self-funded. Your only chance of getting any help with it is to win a (rare) scholarship, persuade someone to sponsor you (difficult) or secure a business-development loan from a bank – usually Barclays or The Co-operative Bank.

Some companies offer directorial training opportunities. The Little Angel Theatre in Islington, 'the home of British puppetry', has a scheme, for example. Each year it appoints and supports an associate artist for whom the position is a directorial training and development opportunity.

Rachel Warr, theatre director, dramaturg and puppeteer, was associate artist at the Little Angel Theatre for 2012, having been artist-in-residence at Middlesex University the previous year.

'I knew almost from infancy that I wanted to do something in the arts, and by the time I was sixteen or seventeen, I'd realised it would be directing,' she said.

During an English Literature degree at Sheffield, where she took part in as much theatre as possible, there was a useful development. Having trained in mime and mask under someone who had trained in physical theatre at the Lecoq school in Paris, she directed an original play which was then chosen to represent the UK at a European festival in Rouen. Clearly very exciting stuff, and she was still only nineteen. She went back to the festival two years later and presented new work there.

Since then she has directed in a range of places, including New Wimbledon Theatre, and done a great deal of studio and site-specific work. Last year she performed as a puppeteer in *Antoine and the Paper Aeroplane* at the Prague Quadrennial Festival. The show was shortlisted for a Total Theatre Award at Edinburgh in 2009 and has since toured to Singapore.

The Young Vic New Directors' Programme provides 'positive and proactive support' to directors in the early stages of their careers and helps them to develop their craft. It's basically a network of young directors which helps to organise opportunities, residencies and other forms of training for young directors.

The Regional Young Directors' Scheme offers director training too. It awards up to three bursaries a year, enabling three directors to spend one year based in a UK theatre. The directors gain experience in all aspects of the theatre's operations and undertake a programme of training to include assisting on productions.

Further reading

Getting Directions: A Fly-on-the-Wall Guide for Emerging Theatre Directors, Russ Hope (Nick Hern Books, 2012)

How to Direct a Play, Braham Murray (Oberon Books, 2012)

So You Want to Be a Theatre Director?, Stephen Unwin (Nick Hern Books, 2004)

Useful websites

Little Angel Theatre www.littleangeltheatre.com

Regional Young Directors' Scheme
www.itvtheatredirectorscheme.org

The Young Vic New Directors' Programme
directors.youngvic.org

Casting Director

What does a casting director do?

A casting director assembles a group of actors who are suitable for a role and presents them to the director and producer to choose from.

That involves talking to agents, doing availability checks, setting up casting sessions, typing 'deal memos' (an informal agreement) and contracts – possibly juggling two or three productions at once. So it's potentially quite stressful.

Some institutions still maintain internal casting departments – the National Theatre, the RSC and the BBC, for example – but most casting directors are independent freelancers running their own offices, expanding their staffing needs on a production-to-production basis.

How do you become a casting director?

Most casting directors start either as a casting assistant or casting associate by working alongside someone with experience. But it is not an easy job to get into. It's all a matter of timing, patience and persistence and getting to know how the industry works. The current edition of *Contacts*, updated and published annually by Spotlight, will help with this.

Paul De Freitas, a former child actor, started work as a casting director aged sixteen and set up his own office when he was twenty-two. 'There is no real training for this work apart from watching actors at work on stage and screen as much as you can,' he says.

He recommends that you train yourself to watch every performance with a casting director's eye and ear. 'Ask yourself how you would cast this actor in other shows. It's a case of getting into the right mindset. I never just watch TV. Even with commercials I am thinking about how they've been or could be cast.'

'Casting directors draw on years of artistic taste, imagination, knowledge, research and political expertise – all this before the collaboration with the director, producer, writer, etc. begins. It is a job that requires an understanding of psychology, artistic taste and style, interpretative taste, current and historical social politics – and, of course, knowing our core subject thoroughly – the different levels and styles of national and international actors and acting. We have to assess the limits to which actors can be pushed artistically, when to take a risk, when to cast against type. It is our job to know them intimately, and to use our knowledge of the wide variety of their skills to conjure up an acting company for a project that allows the visual story to be told. We are constantly interviewing actors, assessing and filtering theatre, film and television performances; often hundreds of actors will be considered for roles before you even set up an audition list.'

From the Casting Directors' Guild website

Some casting directors work first as agents and, according to Paul De Freitas, it helps to have some acting or directing experience, although it isn't essential. 'I've never directed a show but I find myself directing audition sessions,' he says.

Working as a children's casting director

Some casting directors specialise in working with children. Jo Hawes, for example, casts and looks after the children for many of the top London musicals and plays such as *Oliver!* and *The Sound of Music*. Jessica Ronane is responsible for the children in *Billy Elliot the Musical*. Unusually, at the time of writing, Ronane and Hawes are working together on the children's casting for the RSC's *Matilda the Musical*.

One of the complications of working with children is that there has to be three or four teams to cover eight shows a week, as children may, by law, work only for a very limited time each week. And Hawes has to spend a lot of time obtaining children's licences to work from the local authorities in which the children live. There are also issues with finding suitable accommodation in London for performing children from all over London, as well as working with chaperones.

'I began in 2003, two years before the show opened, by creating a massive, nationwide database of dance schools, clubs, teachers and so on, and then began to trawl. And we still work in the same way.

Each summer around six to eight boys are brought to London for an intensive summer school lasting five to six weeks. They live in the large 'Billy House', which is rented by the company in a leafy London suburb. The children sleep in dormitories, and are looked after by houseparents. They have workshops each afternoon and the progress they make is astounding.

From this group, some boys emerge as the new Billys. We watch them carefully and observe their commitment, attitude and stamina, as well as their dance and, to a lesser extent, singing and acting ability as they progress through the audition process. Then final decisions are confirmed by the show's choreographer, Peter Darling, who deliberately doesn't see the boys in development.

Since the average boy works on the show for two years, the company also has to ensure that his own education needs are met. We have two tutors and classrooms in the Billy House. The tutors liaise closely with the boys' schools to make sure that they don't lose out, and that they make the academic progress expected of them – and more. Some of the parents see this one-to-one teaching as a real bonus.'

Jessica Ronane, Children's Casting Director,
Billy Elliot the Musical

Further reading

Children in Theatre: From the Audition to Working in Professional Theatre, Jo Hawes (Oberon Books, 2012)

Useful websites

Casting Directors' Guild www.thecdg.co.uk

Paul De Freitas www.pauldefreitas.com

Musical Director

What does a musical director do?

Any show that includes musical performance has a musical director – or MD. He or she rehearses and leads the live music.

The job usually includes developing performance with solo or group singers (although there may be assistants such as chorus masters to do the spade work with groups), and conducting or leading the band or orchestra at every performance. Unlike the director, the MD usually has a hands-on role – often visible and certainly audible – at every performance, although sometimes a conductor is present to act as a musical supervisor if the MD isn't conducting him or herself.

Sometimes the music is pre-recorded rather than played live, which is a much cheaper option for the producer than having to pay players every night. If recorded music is used, it will be the MD who has overseen it and rehearsed the music with the performers.

How do you become a music director?

Music directors are almost always former instrumentalists who have studied music to a high level. Small bands are often led from the keyboard by the MD. Larger ones are conducted. Many MDs have played in pit bands or performed on stage so that they know what an MD does and how he or she works.

Some musical-theatre courses have modules which develop MD skills, and there are a few postgraduate training opportunities (at LAMDA, for example) for musicians who want to move towards directing.

Further reading

The Musical Director's Handbook, Stuart Morley (Authors OnLine, 2012)

Other Directors

What other areas need directors?

Some shows will have other subsidiary directors such as fight or movement directors (sometimes called choreographers) liaising with the director. Obviously, this depends on the nature of the show and the size and budget of the company.

How do you become a movement director?

Movement directors are people responsible for how performers move in the playing area. It is quite likely to include teaching and developing dance, but can include other sorts of movement such as acrobatics. When Antony Sher played the title role in *Tamburlaine the Great* for the RSC (directed by Terry Hands), there was an almost unbelievable scene in which Sher delivered a long speech while hanging upside down from a rope – a theatrical device which would have needed a lot of support from a skilled movement director.

There are courses at all levels in choreography – from classes at local further-eduction colleges through to full-blown degrees. Most of these are underpinned by dance with scope to develop into other areas, including combat.

How do you become a fight director?

There are qualifications in elementary combat which most actors obtain as part of their drama-school training. Combat classes are taught by experienced combat directors such as Kevin McCurdy at Royal Welsh College of Music and Drama, and Nicholas Hall at East 15 Acting School.

If this sounds an appealing job, train in lots of fighting techniques, martial arts and acrobatics. The more styles and different kinds of physical arts and stunts you are capable of, the better. Train for several years so you are not just proficient but really good at what you do.

Many fight directors began as dancers because both skills are about strength and movement. Most have acting or other performance experience and the combat specialism gradually emerges.

Playwright

What does a playwright do?

He or she is a maker (a 'wright') of plays – in other words, a writer of scripts.

Most productions have a script – the words written down by a dramatist which form the play or show. In most cases, this is the starting point for the director, actors and backstage team.

If the show begins as a devised piece, once the improvising or devising process is complete, the play will usually be 'fixed' in a written form – which it is someone's job to create.

Occasionally, a play without words comes along – especially these days if it's a show for very young children such as Rochdale-based M6 Theatre Company's *One Little Word* or, in Tower Hamlets, Half Moon Theatre Company's *Rip, Fold and Scrunch*. The 'script' of a wordless play consists of a detailed account of what the performers should do – effectively, stage directions without dialogue. It still has to be written, though.

A play, written by a modern playwright, can be:

- An entirely new work with invented characters and plot, e.g. Alan Bennett's *People* or Jez Butterworth's *Jerusalem*.

- Based on characters and events from history, e.g. *The Queen of the North* by Ron Rose or the RSC's *Written on the Heart* by David Edgar.

- A version of a play originally written in another language. Plays by Chekhov, Ibsen and Molière, for example, are performed in English all the time, often in new, updated versions by experts such as Ranjit Bolt or Jeremy Sams. Translator/playwrights usually work from a literal translation so that you don't need to be a Norwegian speaker to write a new version of, say, *Hedda Gabler* in English.

- A reworking of a pre-existing play in a new version. Richard Bean's highly successful *One Man, Two Guvnors* sets Goldoni's 1743 play *The Servant of Two Masters* in 1960s Brighton and scripts it in modern English. Ryan Craig's *How to Think the Unthinkable* is a reworking of Sophocles's *Antigone* for young audiences.

- An adaptation of a novel or other written form, such as a poem. *War Horse* is playwright Nick Stafford's version of Michael Morpurgo's novel.

A playwright's work can certainly take many forms.

Large theatres such as the National have literary departments staffed by people who read, commission and assess new plays – another way of working in theatre.

How do you become a playwright?

There seem to be almost as many routes as there are writers of plays.

The first, and most important thing, is that if you – however young you are – want to write plays, you should see as much theatre as possible and read as many scripts of all kinds as you can. Read or see classics, translations, devised work, new writing, physical theatre, adaptations, comedy, tragedy (and everything in between).

As with most writing (and other) skills, you learn the art of writing plays by doing it. David Edgar, the playwright who founded the MA in Playwriting Studies at the University of Birmingham in 1989, wrote little plays for family and friends for performance in the garden shed from age five. Later he studied drama at Manchester University with the intention of becoming a playwright.

Other veteran playwrights read English at university. Alan Bennett, for example (*The History Boys, The Lady in the Van, People*) went to Oxford. David Hare (*Amy's View, Stuff Happens*) read English at Cambridge. In both cases, they became heavily involved with the university drama scene as undergraduates.

On the other hand, Tom Stoppard (*Arcadia, Rosencrantz and Guildenstern are Dead*) didn't go to university or college at all. He went into journalism when he left school, became a theatre critic and his career as a playwright developed from there.

Some successful playwrights train at drama school as performers and practise their writing skills as they train. There is usually a student or two at every drama-school graduation showcase who has written his or her own material.

Otherwise, for many students wanting to write plays, it is still worth studying drama or English academically at university. Then, if you can afford it, consider one of the postgraduate courses that specialise in playwriting. Sarah Kane, Fraser Grace, Helen Blakeman and Sarah Woods did the University of Birmingham course mentioned above.

There are several schemes set up to encourage new theatrical writing, such as the Royal Court's Unheard Voices programme, which aims to support and develop writers whose voices are under-represented on British stages. The Royal Court's literary department also reads three thousand unsolicited scripts a year as it searches for vibrant new plays to stage. The same theatre has a studio and Writers' Programme, which works with groups of young writers and mounts the Young Writers' Festival and the Rough Cuts season. The Royal Court has been central to the development of new writing for many years and remains deeply commited.

Soho Theatre is another example of a venue that works very hard actively to seek and develop new writing.

The Bruntwood Prize for Playwriting is a national competition run annually in partnership with the Royal Exchange Theatre in Manchester. There are cash prizes and performance opportunities for winners. Their website offers a great deal of helpful advice.

Rachel De-lahay came to the Royal Court through the Unheard Voices Writers' Programme and was part of the training group aimed at young Muslim writers. Her first play, The Westbridge, *was jointly awarded the Alfred Fagon Award in 2010 while still unproduced. It was then staged at the Royal Court in December 2011 and was warmly received by critics.*

'I trained as an actress at drama school and used skills gained there to have a go at writing something for the first time. I'm sure if I'd have studied scriptwriting at a university or on an accredited course I would have gained an invaluable set of skills, particularly to do with structure and form. As it was, I had to trust that, as an actress, whilst my approach to a script would have been different, my skills were equally valuable.

I find it easy developing characters, giving them wants, objectives, obstacles, and then using improvisation skills as a way to start writing dialogue. Using this to get myself onto a writing course felt like a bit of a lottery. I was aware of extremely talented friends who weren't getting through.

The Royal Court runs about three groups per year and you have no idea if the country's best new writers are all submitting to the same group you are, or whether they applied for a different intake. This is where perseverance pays off. Lots of friends who didn't get onto a course straight away eventually did. There are so many amazing opportunities for new writing at present that I genuinely think in such a tough industry it's best to apply to all of them.

Once in a group, I made the most of it – absorbing as much as I could from all the brilliant practitioners they brought in to talk to us. I was aware how difficult it would be to actually get a play into production and so I used the only tool at my disposal – which was to tell a story only I could tell, to write about a world only I could write. That means that if (when) it's rejected, you have enough faith in its strength to be able to offer it elsewhere.

I'm very aware that I couldn't have orchestrated getting my first play on, nor could I write a template for others to do the same. It was a combination of me writing the strongest story I could, then that story appealing to the personal taste of the artistic director and/or literary manager, whilst also fitting with the theatre's already-programmed pieces. Too much of that was luck.

My life as a playwright is mostly a battle to overcome procrastination at the start of a new commission, panic all-night writing sessions nearer to the deadline of said commission, and fear of not paying the rent on time once that commission has been completed and I'm not sure where my next pay cheque's coming from.

As I know that this is what my life will be for the foreseeable future, I have become pretty smart with money as I genuinely want this to be my only income. Therefore I don't splurge just because my agent has sent me over a nice royalty cheque, which can be a bit sad but then I remind myself I'm getting paid to do a creative job that I love.'

If you want to be a playwright, get involved in all the writing courses for young people you can. Soak it all up. At best you'll learn amazing things, at worst you'll make new friends – there's no such thing as too much experience. But most importantly, make sure you love it. It can easily take you over and if you're not having fun every step of the way, you should give it up and do something else.

Further reading

The Art of Translation, Ranjit Bolt (Oberon Books, 2011)

How Plays Work, David Edgar (Nick Hern Books, 2009)

The No Rules Handbook for Writers, Lisa Goldman (Oberon Books, 2012)

So You Want to Be a Playwright?, Tim Fountain (Nick Hern Books, 2007)

Write a Play – and Get it Performed, Lesley Bown and Ann Gawthorpe (Teach Yourself, 2010)

Useful websites

Bruntwood Prize for Playwriting www.writeaplay.co.uk

Half Moon Theatre Company www.halfmoon.org.uk

M6 Theatre Company www.m6theatre.co.uk

Designer

Everything you see in the production has to be designed: costume, set, props, sound and lighting.

What does a designer do?

Designers come up with ideas relating to how the play looks and, sometimes, sounds. These ideas for sets, costumes, props, lighting and/or other aspects of the play or show are then communicated to the people who make what the designer has specified.

The designers collaborate closely with the director, usually some time before the play goes into rehearsals. Both the designer and the director will have a vision for the play and it is, obviously, vital that these ideas are coordinated.

Suppose, for example, a director decides that she wants to set her production of *Measure for Measure* in twenty-first-century Amsterdam. It is up to the designer to think of ways of getting the look and feel of that right so that it is visually convincing for the audience as soon as they see the set.

When Es Devlin designed Sally Potter's production of *Carmen* for the English National Opera in 2007, she and Potter spent time together in Devlin's house in Spain. They were soaking up the ambience of Spain and developing ideas for the production together.

In a big company, several designers will be employed. If sets, costumes and lighting (among other things) are designed by different people, there will be a lots of liaising and meetings.

If the show is produced on a smaller scale, it is quite common for the whole visual package – sets and costumes, although not usually lighting – to be designed by a single person.

A set designer typically creates a model box (a miniature stage showing all the set pieces and elements of the design) as a way of communicating his or her design. Successful designers sometimes employ model-makers to work on these as a way of saving time.

Model-making is yet another way of working in theatre. Trainee or young designers often work as assistants and/or model-makers with established designers as a way of increasing experience – and paying the bills while, as free-lance workers, they wait for commissions to come in.

Designers of costumes, hats, hairstyles and make-up schemes usually present drawings of what they want, so good draughtsmanship is a useful skill for aspirant designers to develop.

Kate Unwin is a freelance designer. Today she designs fashion as well as set and costume for theatre. She graduated with a first-class degree in interior architecture from De Montfort University, where she specialised in TV scenography.

'I'd never thought of TV scenography before as a career, and it brought together all my interests of design, culture, literature, theatre, film, etc. I was advised to begin in theatre to get into TV, but loved theatre so much I stayed there – although I have done some film work, music videos and educational films.

When I graduated, I worked in the box office of Loughborough Town Hall Theatre part-time, and worked unpaid on set-painting, prop-making, costume, lighting, crewing, follow-spot, etc., to get experience. This got me the job of production assistant at the Haymarket Theatre, Leicester. I had wanted to work there since I saw a production of *Richard III* when I was a student. After about six months, my boss, Graham Lister, asked the education department if they would give me the opportunity to design one of their adult-education shows. They really liked what I did and within a year I was designing *An Ideal Husband* for the main stage. So definitely a case of right place, right time.

Every day is different. I try and get up at 6.30 every day and go for a run – and that clears my head so I can plan what I am going to be doing for the day. Between 8.30 and 9.30, I go through emails and put some updates about work onto social media. I tend to stay at home if I'm at the researching or designing stages as it's where all my books and resource materials are. If I am making sets, costumes or props, then I will be at my studio. I might be sourcing – which means I am going to my suppliers to get fabrics, materials, etc. The evening usually comprises emails, going through lists of things to do, probably a few more hours designing and researching – it never ends!

If you're a teenager wanting to get into design then volunteer, assist, meet people, network. Show enthusiasm and creativity and make yourself available for every opportunity. I wanted to assist on a play called *The King of Spin*, based on *Richard III*, which was performed at Bosworth battlefield. So I put together a research report on Richard III and asked if I could assist. The designer dropped out and I was offered the job. This was in my first year of being a designer.'

Lydia Denno is a freelance set and costume designer. She graduated from Nottingham Trent University in 2007 with a BA (Hons) in Theatre Design.

'My work as a theatre designer means I am responsible for the overall aesthetic of a piece of theatre. This primarily includes the set, costumes and props, although it can extend to video or projection work incorporated into the staging, puppet design and even mask work.

When I left school I was very unsure of what I wanted to do and so, liking art and design, I found myself doing an art foundation year in order to postpone the decision. During that year, I decided to pursue a degree in Theatre Design as it seemed to amalgamate a lot of my disparate interests – I loved spatial design as much as I loved history, and fashion design as much as I loved literature. Theatre Design allowed me to marry all these passions.

The transition from studying to working was essentially a lucky break. One of my final-year projects involved working alongside a professional director who opened lots of doors. It was a last-minute decision to pick that particular project, but on the back of it I was invited to the theatre after graduation to assist on my first professional show.

Like the majority of contemporary theatre designers, I work on a freelance basis which means a lot of variety. I work for theatres all around the country on a wide range of shows.

Typically, I will start a job by reading and becoming very familiar with the script. In close communication with the director and other 'creatives' (writer, sound designers, lighting designers, composers, etc.), an overall vision for the play will be agreed and that's the framework within which I start formulating design ideas. This vision may take into account the moment in history, how naturalistic/surreal the piece is going to be, the environment it takes place in, who the characters are and the audience's relationship to the play.

Following an extensive research period, drawing inspiration from various sources ranging from history to contemporary art to politics, I start to sketch ideas for set, costumes and props. Then comes a three-stage model-making process for the set. A white-card scale model, much like an architect's, is drawn up to communicate the basic spatial ideas, followed by a costing model stage and, eventually, a final model, complete with colour, texture and specific detail. Accompanied by technical drawings, this serves both as a tool for the director and actors to envisage the space they will be playing in, and for the set builders and scenic artists to know how the finished piece should look.

Final costume and prop designs are most often presented as annotated 2D paintings or drawings, with suggestions of fabrics, fastenings, etc.

Once the initial design stage is complete and models and drawings have been approved, the theatre designer's job is to oversee the making process (or in some cases where budget is low, to make it themselves)! As I work with set-builders and costume -makers I see the design ideas coming to life.

The final stage of the process is 'tech week', when the set is brought onto the stage, finishing touches are made and the actors carry out their technical rehearsals in costume. This is often one of the most hectic weeks of the process, as final tweaks are made and technical issues resolved. It culminates in the opening night which is usually (I hope!) one of the most exhilarating moments in the project as your work is revealed to a paying audience for the first time.

It's never too soon to get involved for anyone interested in a design career. I didn't volunteer in my local theatre or seek opportunities to work alongside professional designers, but I see young people doing that now and I think it's invaluable. One of the key things behind success in the theatre industry is the ability to get beside a myriad of people who work there and to have a basic understanding of how important everyone's role is in the process. The best way to learn that is to witness it. Don't be afraid to get hands-on and involved in whatever way you can.

Beyond that, I really do encourage some training in theatre design, whether that be a degree or similar college course. It gives you a good overall understanding of the various aspects of the job, often including the base skills in construction, costume and prop-making, which better inform the design process as well as the critical side of theatre theory.

If you're an aspirant designer you also need to see lots of theatre and to get inspired by as many different visual media as possible. See shows, visit galleries, read books... even watch TV!'

Jean Chan won the Linbury Biennial Prize for Stage Design in 2009. That won her the job of designing the sets for adaptation of Elizabeth Laird's novel *The Garbage King* at Unicorn Theatre the following year. Chan did a foundation course in Art and Design at Coleg Sir Gar, followed by a BA (Hons) in Theatre Design at Royal Welsh College of Music and Drama. Since winning the prize, Chan has worked with Trestle Theatre Company and the Arcola Theatre. She has also been involved with RSC's Young People's Shakespeare productions and with Theatre Centre, among other commissions and assignments.

How do you become a designer?

A number of drama schools have undergraduate courses specifically devoted to design, as Royal Welsh College of Music and Drama does. Rose Bruford College offers a three year BA (Hons) course in Theatre Design. It also runs a BA (Hons) in Lighting Design, and a short summer school in lighting design which anyone interested could use as a taster before deciding whether to apply for the degree programme.

Another option is to go to drama school (or university) and study something more general, and then focus on design at postgraduate level – although you will have to self-fund. Acclaimed designer Es Devlin, for example, read English at Bristol and then trained in design at the legendary – but now closed – Motley Theatre Design Course, founded and run by Margaret 'Percy' Harris until her death in 2000.

RADA is one of the colleges offering postgraduate design courses. It runs a two-year course in Theatre Design (Set and Costume) and a short course each summer with the same title. Then there's a two-year diploma in Sound

Design and a summer course. RADA's Stage Electrics and Lighting Design course is taught over four terms.

Some universities – such as Nottingham Trent and University College Falmouth – run degree courses in theatre design too, but take care and ask questions. Make absolutely sure that there is plenty of practical experience built into the course. Ask how many teaching hours a week you can expect. Bear in mind that drama-school students get at least thirty.

Sound and light have to be designed just as sets, props and costumes do.

Tom Holland is a sound designer, and at the time of writing his most recent production was Love, Love, Love *at the Royal Court. Having done one year of music at university, Tom transferred to Royal Central School of Speech and Drama for the Theatre Sound course – then a fairly new three-year degree.*

'My responsibility is to support any sort of performance production with sound, music or amplification, and to do this while working in collaboration with the director and the rest of the creative team (lights, set, etc.) and/or cast members.

At the beginning, I had no idea that music and sound could be combined to create a career.

The course at Central covered all aspects of sound in theatre, ranging from simple sound-file editing all the way up to delaying speaker systems and working with mics, programming desks, etc. The aspect of the course I found to be the most useful and ultimately rewarding was the practical knowledge gained with working on full-scale public productions during the entire three years.

Today my job mainly involves collaboration. It's the area where people and technology meet in trying to create interesting and dynamic performance elements.

Basically anything an audience hears is down to me. Practically, this might include aspects as diverse as programming music for a nightclub scene in a play, researching Canada Geese flight patterns for an outdoor scene located in North America, or amplifying a stage to recreate the acoustics for a scene in a prison.

The other large part of my job is to manage the way an audience hears all this content. This might include decisions about where speakers are located in a performance area, how loud a sound is to be, and the clarity or integrity of the sound. I believe these are all applicable to any sort of performance, from theatre or opera, to film and live music gigs.

If you want to work in sound, seek out some sort of formal training if possible. I certainly don't think you need a three-year course to get into the profession, but a period of time really learning from people who have worked, or are working, in the job is key.

I believe that having a good solid knowledge of how sound works and how to control/enhance it with the technology now available are the really important factors, as well as having a genuine interest in sound. Having gained this, one is better positioned to apply it to an area of interest (e.g. mixing live bands/musicals, or working in a recording studio).

For example, a sound engineer I know studied studio sound at SAE Institute London but is now touring the world mixing musicals in huge venues.

Having said how important a good basic knowledge of sound is, there is nothing like learning on the job. I believe that, as soon as is practicable, a teenager should look at getting out there and working on as many professional productions as possible.

One year working in professional sound is worth two years of training, I am a firm believer in that.'

Useful websites

SAE Institute London www.london.sae.edu

Kate Unwin www.kateunwin.co.uk

TECHNICAL JOBS

- STAGE MANAGER   64
- TECHNICIANS AND OPERATORS   69
- COSTUME STAFF   73
- MAKE-UP, HAIR, WIGS AND PROSTHETICS STAFF   81
- PROPS STAFF   86
- SCENIC CONSTRUCTION AND PAINTING   93

Stage Manager

What does a stage manager do?

A stage manager is a manager of people. He or she liaises between performers, director and technicians, and is responsible for ensuring that everything runs smoothly and efficiently during rehearsals and performances.

The work requires a lot of calm multitasking and any good stage manager must be able to work under pressure. It often involves long hours and can be very repetitive as well as physically demanding.

> 'You must have the temperament and ability to get along with people in both the artistic and technical sides of theatre, and to understand what they do. It is part of the attraction of the work that each new job will introduce new and different challenges... the stage manager and his or her team should sit at the heart of the production and be the first port of call for anything concerning the show for all those involved in creating and running it.'
>
> *From the Stage Management Association website*

While the show is in rehearsal, the stage manager is the link between the artistic process in the rehearsal room and the people who are physically building, sewing, assembling and making the production elsewhere. He or she is there to prevent *anything* from adversely affecting the production. Hence the emphasis on detail and good communication skills.

Once the show has opened, the stage manager is responsible for the management of each performance. That means ensuring that the production continues to run exactly as directed and designed.

In a large company, the stage manager will lead a team, typically consisting of him or herself and two others: a deputy stage manager (DSM) and an assistant stage manager (ASM).

Each of these has a quite distinct role. The DSM will also generally cue the show, giving calls to the actors and all departments, enabling the coordination of scenery, lighting and sound changes. The ASM will frequently be 'running the wings', which means looking after other backstage aspects, particularly props. On a large show there will be more than one ASM and a team of stagehands.

In a smaller theatre, or during a tour, the stage manager may also have to be 'roadie'. That means driving, loading and unloading vans, putting up the set, and designing and operating both sound and lighting.

Colin King is stage manager (among other things) at Spotlites Theatre, Chatham, Kent

'I was interested in drama at school and got involved with the school play once a year. I got hooked. Then I joined a local youth theatre and did all the backstage things I could.

I applied to several drama schools offering stage management and eventually selected Rose Bruford's Technical Theatre Arts degree. I am continually training and learning as technology and practices evolve – so my training isn't finished yet!

My first job after college was in sound in the West End. After ten years of working on various shows and companies in London as a 'soundy' and a stage manager, I decided to give up the rat race and do something important and less glamorous. I joined a small producing theatre in Chatham where I work now as a stage manager.

As a stage manager for a small producing theatre, I tend to have to do everything that's needed. I change jobs according to each show's needs. Variously, I am sound technician, lighting designer, set builder, IT manager, online box-office supervisor, photocopier man, floor-sweeper, drain-unblocker (and award-acceptor!) as well as my usual stage-manager duties. I have another member of the stage-management team to help me and we can always ask the actors to lend a hand to load the van. We are led by our director as to what she wants in regards to the look and feel of each show, but I usually have a very open brief for the set, lights, etc., and can therefore blend everything easily to fit the design of each show. Currently we specialise in producing children's theatre, which is one of the hardest things to pull off as kids these days are used to the high-tech world of Xbox and CGI cinema. I spend more time working on these shows than I ever did at the RSC.

I know that my role as a stage manager is very different from how it would be in a large organisation, where there are whole departments dedicated to the task to do things "properly" — with a thorough paperwork trail, organising rehearsal schedules, costume-fitting calls, blocking the actors' movements in rehearsals, cueing the light and sound technicians during a show. But "proper" stage management wouldn't work in a company the size of ours. We would be in meetings all day and get nothing done.

Once you're eighteen, you can either try to get a job (or there are apprenticeships popping up) with a small producing theatre and work your way up the ladder, or you can go to a drama school like Rose Bruford and get a three-year course under your belt (mostly degrees nowadays).

It is a hard life. I work up to eighty hours a week on average. It isn't glamorous. No one asks for your autograph. It is a way of life rather than a job, but if it's for you then it is one of the most rewarding ways of living.

Don't be put off at the first rejection you get, keep banging your head against the stage door until someone lets you in!'

How do you become a stage manager?

If you're a teenager wanting to get into stage management, get involved with your school's drama department, join a youth theatre or do the follow-spot at your town's pantomime – get some experience under your belt. Once you know what a 'barn door' is (it's a light), and that a 'half' isn't actually thirty minutes, then get some serious work experience with a producing theatre or a West End show, and see what exactly this stage-managing business is all about.

Many of the major drama schools offer stage-management courses. They are run in conjunction with acting courses and a considerable part of the course is devoted to work on the mounting of college productions. That means that you work with other students and stage-manage the shows that they're presenting as a way of developing your skills.

Several courses incorporate secondment to professional theatres. That means that you begin to build up contacts. It's quite common for stage-management graduates to get offered paid work in the venues they were seconded to once training is complete.

Acting courses, as we shall see in Part Three of this book, usually receive thirty or forty applications for each available place. Stage-management courses are oversubscribed too, but to nothing like the same extent.

There might, for example, be three or four people applying for each place. That means your chances of being offered a place to study stage management are relatively high.

Further reading

Essentials of Stage Management, Peter Maccoy (Methuen Drama, 2004)

Stage Management: The Essential Handbook, Gail Pallin (Nick Hern Books, new edition 2010)

Stage Management: A Practical Guide, Soozie Copley and Philippa Killner (The Crowood Press, 2001)

Useful websites

Stage Management Association
www.stagemanagementassociation.co.uk

Technicians and Operators

What does a lighting technician do?

He or she runs and controls the show's lighting. A lighting designer will have specified how the show should be lit and what effects used.

In a big theatre, or on a big show, the lighting team is responsible for making sure the lighting rig works (which is no mean feat). They will also make sure that the lighting remains consistent with the designer's intentions.

Many modern shows use highly sophisticated, intelligent lights. These are basically robots with very tiny and complex parts, so there are lots of different components to go wrong. Before each performance, lighting technicians carry out a 'rig check', which involves going through every light or piece of electrical equipment in the show to make sure it's working correctly.

They also maintain the kit. This can be as basic as cleaning and keeping it in a good condition, to routinely taking apart giant moving lights and replacing items such as gels. On a big show, there may also be effects such as smoke, haze projection and other special effects – all of which are the responsibility of the lighting team.

On a smaller show or in a touring company, the 'lighting team' may be a single person and the effects may be fewer and simpler, but the principles are the same.

Lighting technicians are often freelance and working on contract. Others are permanently employed in venues so that they manage the lighting for any show which is staged there, including those by touring companies.

How do you become a lighting technician?

Anyone who's interested in lighting needs to get as much hands-on experience as possible by helping with school shows, youth theatre, amateur drama and so on, while still in his or her teens.

After that, most successful lighting technicians study technical theatre in a drama school, college or university, where they specialise in lighting and get plenty more experience working on shows with acting or musical-theatre students.

James Nowell is responsible for the lighting in Matilda the Musical *at the Cambridge Theatre in London, a massive show which, at the time of writing, appears to be settling in for a long future.*

'I did a three-year BA (Hons) in Technical Theatre at Middlesex University in which I mostly chose modules based around lighting and production management (which is now my side project).

At secondary school and college, I had always been interested in technical theatre, often doing most of the lighting for various performing-arts projects. I grew up in Suffolk where there's a thriving arts scene, so I got the chance to be in, and work on, lots of productions.

After graduating in 2007, I did what quite a lot of people do and became a follow-spot operator – in my case on *Chicago*. I got very lucky and managed to move to a full-time position within a few months. Even luckier still, I got moved up again to become number two – deputy lighting director – a year later. I worked hard and gained some great experience on a reasonably simple show. I always continued to work freelance as a production manager outside this full-time job – which I still do. This helped me learn about other shows and theatres which I could apply to my current job.

Matilda the Musical is a huge and amazing show. My responsibilities started with being part of the team that worked out how the show would fit into this venue. Once the show was up, we went into three weeks of technical rehearsals. At this point the director and design teams make changes as well as rehearsing technical elements of the shows with the actors. This can be a very testing period for all. You might spend an hour on a scene – or two days. Changes can be made right up until press night, and sometimes after, so it can take a while for a show to "settle".

We spend a great deal of time in rehearsals with new cast or understudies. And keeping an eye on the focuses of the show is very important. Each light, whether it's a static generic light or a moving light, has a very precise focus on the stage. One moving light may have over a hundred different focuses – and we have lots of those!

It is an incredibly varied job which is one of the best things about it. We have a team of seven, and between us we man five different 'plots' or positions in the theatre.

I think training is very important, but you need to make sure your investment is going to pay you back. I was lucky enough to go to university before the massive rise in tuition fees. Young people now must make sure that their course is right for them.

Even during training, you should look to make contacts and do outside work, even if it's unpaid. Make sure your CV shows good and varied experience.

Be ambitious. Do your best in your full-time job but push yourself outside of it. I've been production-managing other shows since leaving university, but I always make sure I can balance my commitments. Speak to everyone and be confident. Show an interest. If you don't know something, ask. You'll find there are lots of people willing to help out and answer questions.'

As with lighting, a production's sound has to be managed, overseen and operated by a separate individual or team.

Costume Staff

There are a number of different theatre jobs relating to costume. They include:

- Costume designers, as discussed in the previous section.
- Makers of costumes, who need highly developed needlework and artistic skills.
- Wardrobe managers, who look after any stock costumes a company (or drama school) holds.
- Needlework experts, who alter and adapt costumes – often to fit new cast members.
- Dressers, who help actors in productions to change in and out of costumes.

There is often an overlap between the five areas described above. In a small company, one person – typically a freelance – does them all.

Costume is one of the areas of theatre work that provides opportunities for people who don't necessarily have a theatre background. 'Sewing hands', for example, can get work – freelance or as employees – without theatrical experience. Theatre tailors and milliners (hat-makers) have often trained in, or for, the clothing industry and then put their skills to theatrical use.

What do costume staff do?

People who make costumes work to designs. They use fabrics that look authentic – which is very important in a historical show – and learn to cut garments in such a way that the item is practical to wear but looks right. For example, a shirt worn by a male dancer may look like a perfectly ordinary high-street shirt. In fact, most are cut with extra panels in the arms so that the dancer can move his arms freely while the shirt stays in place.

Costume-makers have to understand things such as corsets, crinolines, bustles, codpieces, doublet and hose, and many other historic clothing devices.

Contrary to popular belief, theatrical costumes cannot be a flimsy version of items worn in real life. If anything, they have to be stronger, better made and more robust than ordinary clothes because they get very hard wear on stage – often during a large number of performances.

The usual way of working is for the maker to create paper patterns based on the designs. Fabric is then cut using the paper as a template.

Sewing machines are used a lot, but in a big costume department, such as the one at Glyndebourne Opera in Sussex, there is a lot of hand-sewing and finishing as well. Authenticity is all.

Not that you can generalise too much about costume. The twenty-eight workers in the RSC's costume workshops demonstrate a diverse range of specialist skills. These include, not only tailoring and costume-making, but dyeing, printing, leatherwork, beading, corsetry, millinery, mask-making and jewellery-making, to name but a few.

'There are many routes into a profession within the RSC's costume department. All staff are trained to a high standard. Although some learn these skills on the job, most have a relevant degree-level qualification in addition to specialist professional training.

Alistair McArthur, Head of Costume, originally trained as a stage manager. He worked his way up in the costume field with positions at the Royal National Theatre and the Royal Opera House, in addition to employment as a freelance costume supervisor. "Once you leave any costume-making course, the best thing to do is to find a freelance maker who is willing to take you on as an assistant," he says. "You can only learn so much in a college and you learn much more actually doing the job."'

From the RSC website

But not all costumes are made from scratch for every production – far from it. Big companies hold large repositories of costumes which can be, and routinely are, 'recycled' for future shows.

The staff in charge of these stores do a great deal of laundry, dry-cleaning and repairing to ensure that everything is stored in good, usable condition. They also maintain catalogues and records so that they know exactly what they have and where it is – it's a bit like being a librarian except that you look after costumes instead of books.

Some drama schools have extensive wardrobes and employ staff to run them. They stage student shows all the time but they do not have big budgets, so many costumes come from the store – whose staff will work closely with the show's director, designers and costume-makers, some of whom will be students if these are skills the school runs courses in.

Both RADA and the Royal Conservatoire of Scotland, for example, have very large wardrobes – huge spaces with tightly packed clothes hanging on rails from floor to ceiling, reached by ladders or walkways. They contain thousands of garments, from rows of white shirts, checked sports jackets, black cocktail dresses or pink blouses, through to dinner suits, military uniforms and ballgowns.

Some of these have been made for previous productions. Many are donated, often by people clearing out the home of a deceased relative – things such as 1940s suits or 1920s flapper dresses from Grandpa's or Granny's cupboards are useful acquisitions, for instance.

These departments also hold collections of hats, shoes, bags, belts, costume jewellery and much more.

Lastly, there are still people working backstage in theatres as dressers – although these days it isn't usually much like the situation in Ronald Harwood's 1980 play *The Dresser* which was made into a film in 1983. Harwood had worked as a dresser for Sir Donald Wolfit (1902–1968) and the play is based on his experiences.

These days dressers are usually part of the wardrobe department and the team that deals with storing, racking, cleaning and keeping costumes in good repair. The other main function of the dresser is to ensure costumes are correctly moved and allocated within the theatre, getting them to the correct actors on time and helping the actors get into costume (with the possibility of costume changes within a performance, this is critical). Watch, for example, any pantomime dame – who typically wears eight or nine different, often very elaborate, outfits during the show and needs slick assistance with getting in and out of them at speed.

How do you become someone who works with costumes?

A maker of costumes needs to be a dexterous and attentive creator with a love of clothes and a flair for needlework of all sorts. Being keen on, and interested in, fashion may be an interest which you can angle towards working in theatre.

Anyone who can sew or has some training and/or experience in the clothing or fashion industry could consider applying for basic jobs in costume, with a view to learning specialist theatrical skills on the job. There are also opportunities for people with particular expertise such as corsetry or millinery.

London College of Fashion offers a three-year BA (Hons) in Costume for Performance. Graduates from it have gone on, among many other jobs and roles, to be Head of Wardrobe at *The Lion King*, ladies' maker at Glyndebourne, and menswear maker at the RSC.

Some costume experts train in art schools, many of which now offer specialist courses. Wimbledon College of Art (part of the University of Arts, London), for instance has a BA (Hons) in Theatre and Screen: Costume Interpretation and another in Theatre and Screen: Costume Design.

Some drama schools run specific BA (Hons) degrees in costume. Rose Bruford offers a Costume Production degree. Or there's an intensive two-year vocational and very practical course for four students per year at Bristol Old Vic Theatre School. It covers all aspects of costume work including pattern-cutting, costume-making, costume supervision, dyeing, millinery, corset-making, history of costume, hiring and buying to budget, wig care, basic make-up and all organisational aspects of the work. The students work to given designs, drafting, fixing, making for and dressing all the school's twelve to fourteen public shows and shoots a year.

A number of universities – including Southampton Solent, Huddersfield and Birmingham City – run theatre costume-making degrees too. But, as always, ask the usual questions about how practical the course is, and how much teaching and hands-on experience you can expect.

Sean Barrett is a highly successful theatrical milliner. He made the hats and headdresses for Tim Burton's film Alice in Wonderland, *Joe Wright's* Anna Karenina, *shows such as* Wicked *and* Love Never Dies, *as well as opera and ballet and ITV's* Downton Abbey.

'I did the Theatre Design course at Wimbledon College of Art (where I now teach part-time), and during a taster mini-course in millinery in the first year, I fell in love with hats. A eureka moment. After that I worked on hats in every spare moment and did as much research as I could into millinery and its history.

After college, I worked as an assistant in London Festival Ballet's costume department and continued to practise my hats in the evening. Then, wanting something more creative than my day job, I wrote – with terrific cheek – to the millinery departments of top London stores including Harrods and Harvey Nichols. I was extraordinarily lucky because I actually got work and worked in fashion for a year or so.

Then one day I was chatting to the buyer in one of "my" stores, when the designer for an early Helena Bonham Carter film, *Lady Jane* came in. The buyer, who'd always said my work was very theatrical, introduced us and that became my first film. And everything went from there.

I've never had to look for work and sometimes there's so much it gets very stressful and I have to buy in help, although I'm at my happiest in my bottom-of-the-garden workshop stitching and glueing with the radio on.

My advice to anyone wanting to do theatrical millinery is to head for art school. At the same time, get knowledgeable about hats of all types from all periods. Study books in the library and effigies on tombs. Go to museums. Look at paintings. Think about materials and how they're used. Read and read and read. Then, after college, try to get some work experience in a big company such as the Royal Opera House, National Theatre, RSC or Glyndebourne.

And don't underestimate the importance of charm, good manners and passion. People in the industry are generally very willing to help anyone who's really committed and has the right attitude.'

In many companies and on many shows, jobs such as costume-making, make-up, props and scenic construction are done by the same people. You are unlikely to get, at least at first, enough work in any one of them to keep you going. By all means have a specialism, but be prepared to diversify in order to stay in work. If you can make a convincing wedding cake, then you can probably also paint a flat, apply make-up or run up a dress – or at least assist in doing so. For a maker in theatre, it's a case of the more skills, the better.

Further reading

Patterns for Theatrical Costumes, Katherine Strand Holkeboer (Drama Book Publishers, 1993)

Making Stage Costumes, Tina Bicat (The Crowood Press, 2001)

Useful websites

London College of Fashion www.fashion.arts.ac.uk

Royal Shakespeare Company www.rsc.org.uk

Wimbledon College of Art www.wimbledon.arts.ac.uk

Make-up, Hair, Wigs and Prosthetics Staff

Very few make-up artists and hairdressers are employed in theatre – although specialists are employed in film. Often, a make-up expert is brought in simply to train the cast in how to apply their own make-up or to style hair for the show. Then his or her job is finished.

There are, however, people designing make-up for shows such as *Shrek the Musical, The Phantom of the Opera* or *The Lion, the Witch and the Wardrobe*. Much of the hair and make-up is not naturalistic and needs specialist knowledge.

In many shows, modern actors wear little or no make-up. Now that thrust stages and theatre-in-the-round are such common configurations, the audience is often very close – so old-fashioned, heavy stage make-up will not do. In the past, 'caked on' make-up, for example, was often used mainly to conceal a wig line. But wigs are now made of more sophisticated materials which make them much less obvious. Lighting techniques can also be used, instead of make-up, to make a character look, say, haggard, suntanned or ill.

On the other hand, a big company such as the National Theatre, Royal Opera House or RSC, many of whose shows are elaborately historical, will have a large wig and make-up department.

'Our repertoire regularly calls for blood and gore, fairies and fantastical beasts, and a whole range of other special effects so the department is always busy.'

From the RSC website

What does a make-up or wigs artist do?

Artists work with performers in the hours before a show as they arrive for their scheduled wig and/or make-up calls.

During a performance, a wig or make-up person may be in the wings, in the backstage area or even under the stage, waiting to apply make-up or adjust a hairstyle during a quick change.

Before a play reaches the stage, the wigs and make-up team meet with the designer, director and actors to discuss the look required for each role.

At the RSC, for each production a folder is made up which contains design notes, reference sheets and photographs that will ensure the actor will have the same hair or make-up for every performance. For example, in productions of *The Tempest*, the role of Caliban often requires bright body paint. Photographs are used to help the make-up artist recreate the same look every night.

Sandra Smith is Head of Wigs and Make-up for the RSC.

'When I take on staff, I look for good experience in hairdressing and someone with an artistic eye. Competiton work is also useful as it teaches you to work under pressure and to a deadline.'

There are also, of course, people who make wigs in work-shops – a specialist branch of hairdressing which requires good eyesight, flair and the ability to work to designs.

Prosthetics – such as a long nose for Cyrano de Bergerac or Pinocchio, a fat suit for Falstaff, or horns for characters in Eugène Ionesco's *Rhinoceros* – are usually made in work-shops and tend to link prop-making with make-up skills, so knowledge of both is useful.

How do you become someone who works with make-up, hair, wigs and/or prosthetics?

First you have to learn how to do it so that you can build up a portfolio and demonstrate that you have the required skills.

Some people learn on the job through apprenticeships and training positions – or even unpaid work experience. You can learn a great deal from watching a practitioner at work even if, to begin with, you just wash the brushes and make the tea. Someone who is willing to start in a very menial role, and do it cheerfully, can acquire a lot of useful skills and knowledge.

The London College of Fashion offers a three-year BA (Hons) degree in Make-up and Prosthetics for Perform-ance. LCF also offers a range of industry-based short courses, typically full time for two weeks, or taught over three months or so on Saturdays.

People who have a flair for, or an interest in, hair and make-up might also consider the short course at Greasepaint Make-Up School in Ealing. It runs a very practical fourteen- to fifteen-week course in make-up for TV, film and theatre. There's an option to add two further weeks to work on prosthetics.

'We're extremely lucky to have worked on our own dramas with a TV crew during the course. It's been a brilliant insight into what's expected of us when we leave the comfort of the school and enter this fast-paced industry. It's been a fantastic experience to work with director David Tucker and the actors in a professional environment. Although a little daunting, the challenge has been exhilarating!'

Catherine Burton, Lucy Shelton and Hannah Paul, at the end of a Greasepaint course in 2011.

Delamar Academy in West London runs various make-up courses including a one-year, full-time option, accredited by Middlesex University, and a six-week course on advanced prosthetics.

Another possibility is Brushstroke. Based at Shepperton Studios, its courses include a two-year full-time option, and a nine-month course. The school teaches both modern and period make-up, hair and wig dressings, and runs an agency to help the completers of its courses to find suitable work.

Manchester-based Wigs Up North provides wigs and make-up for stage and screen, as well as functioning as a training school to teach the skills to others.

Alternatively, there are performance make-up courses in many further-education colleges including West Thames, Coleg Gwent, James Watt and Belfast Metropolitan.

Useful websites

Brushstroke www.brushstroke.co.uk

Delamar Academy www.delamaracademy.co.uk

Greasepaint Make-Up School www.greasepaint.co.uk

London College of Fashion www.fashion.arts.ac.uk

Royal Shakespeare Company www.rsc.org.uk

Wigs Up North www.wigsupnorth.co.uk

Props Staff

What do props staff do?

Props are properties – movable items used on stage during the course of the action. They include things such as the teacups in *The Importance of Being Earnest*, the books Matilda reads in *Matilda the Musical*, the flower Puck brings back for Oberon in *A Midsummer Night's Dream*, and the basket of figs concealing the asp in *Antony and Cleopatra*.

Many of these props are specially made by trained craftspeople. Others are sourced from second-hand shops, eBay – and even, occasionally, from refuse skips. Designers make it clear what is required and, one way or another, the props department, often in liaison with the stage-management department, will produce the item.

Just as they do with costumes, large companies and drama schools have a props repository – which resembles a very well-organised gigantic bric-a-brac store, containing all sorts of unlikely items such as the odd skull (for *Hamlet*), severed head (for *Macbeth*), or the 'almost any play' plates of fake food – along with coal scuttles, classical busts and clocks from every era. Obviously, it is someone's job to manage all this and to know exactly what's there.

But many props – along with masks and puppets – are made in workshops. Makers use metal, fibreglass, plastic, soft materials, wood and many other materials, all of which they have to learn how to handle.

A prop-maker needs a wide range of skills, including sculpting, carpentry, sewing, welding, papier mâché, sign-writing, metal-casting and computer-aided design (CAD).

On the job, you:

- Work from rough drawings or detailed three-dimensional designs.
- Have to do research to make sure your prop is right for the historical period or situation.
- Experiment with different materials to get the best results.
- Use many different tools – anything from a needle to an oxyacetylene welder.
- Adapt, change or repair ready-made articles.
- Source or buy props.
- Ensure that props are usable and resilient enough to last for the run of the show.
- Work with stage managers, production designers, set designers and builders, wardrobe staff and model-makers.

Some of the biggest theatre companies employ construction specialists as members of staff. The National Theatre, for example, has a permanently staffed props workshop. But smaller companies hire freelance craftspeople to work short-term on specific productions. Most theatre craftspeople are therefore freelance rather than employees.

In a smaller company, fewer people are involved with the production because there is less money available. So there is necessarily less specialism backstage. One technician might, for example, find him or herself building and painting the scenery as well as making or acquiring the props – and even creating a puppet if that's what the show requires. That is why every technician needs a range of skills.

Puppet-makers are specialised prop-makers. Puppets are increasingly important and commonplace in the theatre industry. No longer do they belong exclusively to theatre for children and young audiences. Puppets are now extensively used in shows such as *War Horse* and *Avenue Q*. The Little Angel Theatre in Islington – like Norwich Puppet Theatre and the Harlequin Puppet Theatre at Rhos-on-Sea in North Wales – specialises entirely in puppetry-based theatre.

Some puppet-makers go on to perform with their creations, but many more make puppets in a workshop and then hand them over to someone else to bring to life on stage.

A professional puppet-maker:

- Uses drawing, design, sculpture and animation skills.

- Works in wood, latex, fabrics and other material (Wallace and Gromit are made of plasticine!).

- Makes many different sorts of puppets, including marionettes, glove, tabletop and rod puppet, as well as moving dolls and animal models.

- Can help to entertain (or even educate) adults as well as children.

- Collaborates with performers and operators.

How do you become a props manager or maker?

You can go to college – usually a drama school alongside actors and other performers – to train in these skills. The training involves a lot of practical work and you will make props, paint scenery and so on for student productions. Most courses run for two years and lead to a diploma in technical theatre.

Royal Central School of Speech and Drama offers an unusual puppetry degree: three-year BA (Hons) Theatre Practice: Puppetry.

Some further-education colleges offer diploma and other courses in technical theatre for sixteen- to nineteen-year-olds. Kingston College in the London Borough of Kingston upon Thames, for example, runs a two-year extended diploma course in Performance Arts which includes props. You can combine this course with GCSE English and Maths and various A level options relevant to performing arts if you wish.

Technical courses usually involve a block of time in which you are out of college attached – or 'seconded' – to a professional theatre. This valuable work experience – generally unpaid because it is part of your training – gives you the opportunity to work alongside, and learn from, professionals who have been doing the job for a long time.

In most cases, you enrol on a general technical course in which you learn stage management, sound and lighting skills, as well as props and other aspects of construction. There is usually an option to specialise later in the course.

Instead of going to college, you might be able to train on the job through an apprenticeship in a theatre. Creative and Cultural Skills, part of the National Skills Academy, promotes and supports apprenticeships in all areas of technical theatre.

Amy Carroll has made props and built sets for many shows, including Father Brown, Doctors *and Birmingham Rep's UK tour of* The Snowman.

'I trained at Trinity University College, Wales, in its Theatre Design and Production department. This was my first insight really into the theatre world. I knew, from earlier training, how to design interiors and I knew how to be in a show, but I didn't know the ins and outs of making a theatre production. Looking back now I wish I had gained more experience in the backstage side of theatre before embarking on a course, as there was a lot to learn initially. There were only nine people on my course which at the time didn't seem odd, but now I realise what a great opportunity that was when I speak to people who were in very large classes and never got to fully realise their designs and creations because of it taking too much time. With our course, the department created a small theatre company and every design we created was fully realised and put to the test so that we could work together as a team to iron out any problems.

For my third year of training, I transferred to CSUF (Californian State University, Fullerton) in the USA. This was definitely an eye-opener! The vast array of things they had to offer was immense and their budgets were unlike anything I had ever seen. This gave me the opportunity to create sets and props I would never have had the budget for in the UK. It broadened my horizons and made me realise that, when you are the designer, the sky is the limit, anything that you can imagine can be created and there will always be someone there in the theatre willing to try and create new and inventive pieces.

After I graduated in 2008, I started working for NTC (Northumberland Theatre Company) as its design assistant, and a year later I travelled back to the USA to work at Stagedoor Manor, a camp in the USA for theatre professionals and students alike. Even though this was the hardest and longest hours I have ever worked, it was definitely an experience that I will value as a massive turning point in my career. I would recommend this for any graduate student of theatre.

Since then I have worked for Birmingham Rep in set and props construction, as a freelance designer/maker and I am just about to start working at the RSC as a stage and props technician.

Prop-making involves anything you could possible imagine, any medium there is. You can make props from almost anything: wood, metal, plastic or latex. You name it – I have made a prop from it! I usually work on a freelance basis making a lot of puppets and wooden props.

If I am designing the items myself, I meet with the director and maybe writers, and the overall designer if there is one. We work out what needs making and then work alongside the concept to create something that fits perfectly within the show. There is often a lot of trial and error in the making process. Usually I am asked to make all manner of weird and wonderful props and I just try testers of as many media as possible to find the one that is perfect for the item I am creating.

There are fewer opportunities now for newcomers because of Arts Council cuts. If you want to make props, I would advise you to find a course in prop-making or theatre design in general. Try and get as much work experience as possible too.

I learned that doing a lot of things for free whilst training can lead to jobs once you have graduated. Working in little workshops and assisting designers is one of the best things I ever did!'

Further reading

Making Stage Props, Andy Wilson (The Crowood Press, 2003)

Stage Source Book: Props, Gill Davies (Methuen Drama, 2004)

Useful websites

Creative and Cultural Skills (National Skills Academy) (www.ccskills.org.uk)

Kingston College www.kingston-college.ac.uk

Royal Central School of Speech and Drama www.cssd.ac.uk

Scenic Construction and Painting

Every show has a designed set. It can be very simple but even an apparently empty space has been designed and has to be managed. On a big show, such as a large West End musical or a full-scale opera, the set can be very elaborate and need a lot of building.

What does a scenery builder do?

Scenery builders – the work is often called scenic construction – are skilled in carpentry, structural design, metal-work and engineering. They build scenery, usually in a workshop, to other people's designs.

The job involves:

- Using hand tools as well as routers, jigsaws, sanders and more elaborate powered carpentry equipment.

- Adapting and making use of welding and cutting techniques for metal.

- Making automated scenery.

- Creating flats and backdrops.

- Paying careful attention to health-and-safety rules.

- Working with others in a team to create illusion in a live show.

What does a scenic artist do?

A scenic artist has to paint – or otherwise appropriately decorate or embellish – backdrops and moveable scenery such as 'flats' for theatre sets, films and concerts. He or she needs skills such as painting, life-drawing, scaling-up, marbling, ragging, spraying, texturing and wood-graining.

The job involves:

- Scaling-up designers' small-scale drawings and models.

- Often operating in a very large studio, because backdrops, which are sometimes on rollers and painted in sections, can be huge.

- Using a paintframe.

- Paying close attention to health-and-safety issues.

- Having the opportunity to work on a wide range of productions.

Big companies have specialist workshops dealing with, for example, armoury. As usual, people who work in small companies often have to be Jacks (or Jills) of all trades. So, in general, the more skills you have, the better.

How do you get to be a scenic constructor or scenery painter?

There are three main ways of training for backstage construction work in the performing-arts industry.

The first is to train in a drama school as a higher-education student. For most students, higher eduction – in universities and colleges – comes at eighteen-plus after A levels or similar post-sixteen work. Most courses are two-year diploma or three-year degrees.

All higher-education stage-management courses in drama schools – such as the two-year diploma course at London

Academy of Music and Dramatic Art (LAMDA) – include some construction training. Royal Conservatoire of Scotland, for instance, runs a very full BA course in Technical and Production Arts. Birmingham School of Acting offers a degree in Stage Management which explores all aspects of technical theatre.

Other courses allow you to specialise from the outset. For example, at RADA there are two-year certificate courses in Scenic Art, Scenic Construction and Property Making. Rose Bruford College runs a three-year degree course in Scenic Arts.

Scenery painters are usually skilled artists who have studied fine arts in art schools, many of which now operate as part of a university. Central St Martins, for example, now in a magnificent converted granary behind Kings Cross Station, is part of the University of the Arts, London.

Further reading

Scenic Art and Construction: A Practical Guide, Emma Troubridge and Tim Blaikie (The Crowood Press, 2002)

Useful websites

Central St Martins College of Art and Design
www.csm.arts.ac.uk

Other Training Opportunities

There will soon be a wide range of backstage training opportunities at The Backstage Centre – Creative and Cultural Skills's centre for training at the High House Production Park in Thurrock, near the Dartford Crossing (www.nsa-ccskills.co.uk/careersadvice). At the time of writing, the purpose-built new building is well on its way. It will offer practical and extensive training and rehearsal space in a bespoke environment offering 'full-scale-venue-style training opportunities'.

Queen's Theatre Hornchurch (www.queens-theatre.co.uk), a professional producing theatre in Essex (London Borough of Havering), runs a twice-yearly work-experience week for fifteen students in school years 10 and 11. It offers the opportunity to explore a range of careers opportunities by working with directors, stage managers, set designers, technicians, artists and a wide range of other professionals, so that participants gain a real understanding of 'pathways into the industry'. The group also develops skills and works together as a company presenting a piece of devised theatre to family and friends at the end of the week. This really is a very useful scheme. If you don't live in the Hornchurch area, approach your local professional theatre and talk to them about work experience, or ask your teachers to make the approach. If enough people are interested, it might be possible to persuade other theatres to do something similar.

ADMINISTRATIVE

In this chapter we'll look at the roles of people who do various sorts of behind-the-scenes work in theatres. Some, but by no means all, of their work is office-based. Much of it is also creative. Nearly everyone working in theatre needs the ability to communicate well with others, and in some cases that includes the public.

- PRODUCER   98
- FRONT OF HOUSE   103
- PUBLICITY   109

Producer

A producer is a person or company responsible for all the business aspects of getting a show on – in close collaboration with artists of all sorts. A producer's role is complex, varied and difficult to generalise about. James Seabright, who has produced over a hundred shows in the West End, on UK and international tours and at the Edinburgh Festival Fringe, summarises this as being in charge of 'delivering a good show, on time and in budget'.

A producer can be one person with an idea who spends (or raises) a small amount of money and works, say, with two or three college friends to mount a couple of performances of a piece of devised work in a low-budget venue. At the other end of the scale, it can be a massive, well-established, highly successful company worth many millions of pounds, such as Cameron Mackintosh Ltd. Sometimes, over many years, the former develops into the latter. Cameron Mackintosh was once a young individual with an overwhelming determination to produce musicals.

Some venues – such as Queen's Theatre Hornchurch, Chichester Festival Theatre or Theatre Royal Bath – produce most or all of the work that plays in their theatres. The National Theatre, Royal Opera House, RSC and similar companies produce much of their own work, but also occasionally co-produce.

Smaller venues and companies often collaborate as producers to spread the cost of a show. It is common to see the names of two or three organisations listed as producers in theatre programmes.

For example, the 2012 pantomime, *Sleeping Beauty*, at the Marlowe Theatre, Canterbury, was co-produced by Marlowe Theatre and Evolution Pantomimes, suggesting that costs (and profits) were shared.

What does a producer do?

The producer – or producing team – must start with an idea, perhaps for a performance of a classic text, or a piece of devised work, or new writing. Or, if the idea involves using a text in copyright, the producer negotiates the rights to it.

Then the producer plans a budget and raises the money. Some drama schools – RADA, for instance – give students practice at this by assigning them a production task and very small budget. One or two in the group will act as producer while the rest perform and provide technical support.

Outside a drama school, the producer will probably be the person who works out what a feasible budget is. He or she must also book a venue or tour, and deal with all the practical details that involves.

He or she brings together performers, directors, designers and backstage people. If the show is very small, some of these jobs will be done by the same people. But each function has to be covered and that's part of the producer's job.

In a small company, the producer is usually directly responsible for marketing or selling the show to make sure that an audience buys tickets and a return is generated on the investment. A larger company or venue will have a marketing manager or department – and we'll discuss that separately later.

Large companies – such as the National Theatre – employ specialist in-house staff to deal with production. In smaller ones, such as Shared Experience or Complicite, production is part of a wider administration role for company managers.

How do you become a producer?

Most producers start by doing it and learning as they go along.

Many is the enterprising, well-organised and motivated individual who has mobilised a small group of fellow students – even when still at school, or in some form of further or higher education – to get a show on the road to the Edinburgh Festival Fringe.

You need step-by-step guidance from a good book about producing and/or from someone who has the experience of having done it and who can advise you about pitfalls and sensible practice.

Alternatively, armed with whatever qualifications you have in the performing arts and/or business (or, perhaps, an unrelated subject), look for a clerical or administrative job with one of the big producing companies and work your way up as you gain experience and knowledge.

Be prepared, though, to start with unpaid work experience or an internship.

'Go out and produce a show. And if it isn't a great show, you learn from it and do another one. If that's a great show, you make the next one bigger and better. Producing is addictive and when you have built valuable relationships with writers, directors, actors and designers, it becomes easier to imagine where the next one might come from.'

James Seabright, Seabright Productions

Sarah Gee formed Filskit Theatre Company to produce shows in 2011 with two other young women. They were all recent Rose Bruford graduates. The trio is Filskit's core cast. The company's first show, Snow White, *toured and was favourably reviewed in 2012. Since then it has developed other work for children.*

'When we first decided to form a company together, it was because we wanted to create and perform work that we enjoyed and found interesting. Once we had started to create shows, we also had to find a way of getting audiences to see them. The transition from being devisers and performers to being producers happened quite organically for us. We found that we started to do the job of a producer without even realising it. We decided to continue to produce our own performances because we feel that, in order to sell the work to venues and audiences, you have to be passionate about it. Who better to do that than the people who create and perform the work?

For us, when we have our producer hats on, we concentrate on making and developing contacts in the industry. We spend a lot of time researching venues and festivals, and contacting them to introduce our company and our work. We also have to read and fill out applications for performance and funding opportunities, read and sign performance contracts and attend meetings with venue programmers.

The most valuable lessons that we have learnt about being producers have come from meetings with industry professionals. In our experience, as long as you show a willingness to learn, programmers and producers are very accommodating and happy to meet for a chat about their work and give helpful hints about "making it" in the theatre industry. It is worth researching companies or venues that you find interesting and contacting them to see if they would be willing to meet and answer some questions about what they do.'

Further reading

The Edinburgh Fringe Survival Guide, Mark Fisher (Methuen Drama, 2012)

How to Produce a West End Show, Julius Green (Oberon Books, 2012)

Management and the Arts, William J. Byrnes (Focal Press, 4th edition 2008)

So You Want to Be a Theatre Producer?, James Seabright (Nick Hern Books, 2010)

Useful websites

Cameron Mackintosh Ltd www.cameronmackintosh.com

Edinburgh Festival Fringe www.edfringe.com

Filskit Theatre Company www.filskittheatre.com

Seabright Productions www.seabrights.com

Front of House

Front of house (FOH) is the area of the theatre which the public sees. It includes foyers, bars, lavatories, cloakrooms, the box office and the auditorium.

Front-of-house jobs include box-office staff, programme sellers, ticket checkers, catering, cloakroom, cleaning, people to help audience members find their seats, and a front-of-house (or simply 'house') manager – who is in charge of all this.

What do front-of-house staff do?

The delegation of jobs and who does what varies from theatre to theatre. To a large extent, obviously, the details depend on the size of the building or company.

Sara Surnam is Customer Services Manager at the Theatre Royal, Bury St Edmunds, having started there twelve years ago as a part-timer in the box office selling tickets. She then became box-office manager. Her job still includes box office. 'Today I'm in charge of all the "customer facing" areas of the building,' she says, adding that the theatre also employs an Operations Manager who, with his own technical staff, is responsible for maintenance.

She oversees all the events that take place in the theatre, and does all the ordering of consumables such as sweets and ice creams. There are thirteen paid staff and sixty volunteer stewards and ushers who report to her – many of them are local sixth-formers wanting to find out if working in theatre is for them.

Ric Garder also works at the Theatre Royal, Bury St Edmunds as Customer Services Officer and, effectively, the Deputy Manager.

The theatre, which was built in 1819 and now fully restored (after many dark years as a beer warehouse for the local brewery which still owns it), has heritage to be managed. The National Trust leases the building and maintains it, and Ric Garder liaises with the National Trust which runs tours of the building four days a week.

Garder also manages occasional lettings of the building, usually on Sundays, for weddings, corporate events, annual meetings and so on. The building, primarily a weekly receiving house, is available to the community and runs four annual summer schools for young people. The job Garder does includes working as duty manager for two shows a week and training other duty managers from amongst the staff.

At York Theatre Royal, which is a larger regional theatre, Kaeli Wishart manages the whole front-of-house operation except the box office, and has sixty-four staff answerable to her, including people in the café and two bars, six duty managers and a seventh who is also her deputy, seven cleaners, more than twenty ushers and four stage-door staff. An archaeology graduate who had worked in museums, she started at the theatre as an assistant manager, having seen a local advertisement, and was later promoted. She has been at York Theatre Royal for thirteen years.

In a very large arts complex, such as the Barbican Centre in London – a completely different sort of organisation from, say, Theatre Royal, Bury St Edmunds – a team of box-office staff works solely on ticket sales, as they do at York Theatre Royal, but this is on much bigger scale. The centre itself has a team of managers, one of whom will be on duty when the centre is open. Someone is also on duty to run the centre's separate areas, such as the concert hall, theatre and cinemas.

Large numbers of people are employed to make sure that events run smoothly and safely.

How do you become front-of-house staff?

Many front-of-house staff start as volunteers. Almost all theatres – including Shakespeare's Globe, whose stewards are volunteers – have opportunities for reliable people willing to get involved and give some time to help make the organisation run smoothly. A good starting point is to volunteer as a programme or ice-cream seller or as an usher. You will probably see most of every show you're working at and you will find out how theatres operate. You will also – useful lesson – find out whether this really is something you'd like to do in the future. There's nothing to be ashamed of in trying it out and deciding that you don't like it after all.

Many universities now run degrees in arts management which might be useful, although a pervading interest in theatre and general administrative efficiency are probably more important. You are dealing with the public directly, so you need verbal confidence. Charm helps too because you will sometimes have to deal with awkward customers.

'I learned this job as I went along,' says Sara Surnam. 'There is no specific qualification for it, although some of the available degrees in arts management and related subjects will cover some aspects. Students on those courses often get opportunities to do internships and placements which can be a way in.'

Ric Garder worked in retail before going to the Theatre Royal, initially as an intern – a route he recommends to anyone wanting to start in any form of theatre management.

York Theatre Royal runs a 'takeover' scheme in which school students and people under twenty-five shadow staff to learn what they do and then programme an event of their own. 'And staff here are always willing to help younger people interested in working in theatre,' says Kaeli Wishart, who also suggests you need to research carefully and approach the right people if you seriously want to pursue career options.

Front-of-house jobs are sometimes advertised in local papers or in the professional press such as *The Stage*. Management jobs in very big venues command high salaries and go to experienced people. Such posts are likely to be advertised in national newspapers or on equivalent websites – something to aim for, perhaps, when you've been at it for a while.

Other front-of-house jobs

It may not be glamorous but someone has to clean the toilets – and the rest of the front-of-house space. While working as a cleaner is not likely to be the lifelong ambition of many readers of this book, it is another starting point. It's the sort of work that could be fitted in alongside another job or college course because it is often done early in the morning or late at night on a part-time basis. And it's yet another way of getting a toe in the building.

No one can afford to be 'above' cleaning anyway. Lack of it is one of the first things the public will notice and complain about, so it's very important. I have seen duty managers hoovering or mopping up in an emergency. Cleaning is something everyone working in theatre needs to be able to do if necessary.

Cloakroom management is another important and responsible job, because you are looking after theatregoers' possessions. Cloakroom staff are needed only for the duration of a performance and a margin either side of it, so there is obviously scope for part-time work or volunteering here.

Nearly all theatres serve refreshments of some sort. It might be an all-day café also used by the non-theatregoing public, such as the ones at the Lighthouse in Poole or West Yorkshire Playhouse in Leeds. Or it might be just a small bar open before the show for an hour and during the interval. Whatever sort of outlet it is, it has to be staffed.

Some in-theatre cafés are contracted out so staff are employed by another company rather than by the theatre – although staff, crucially, are still on the premises and working, in the broadest sense, in theatre.

If you love catering and have always wanted to do it professionally but you are also keen on theatre, this could be an imaginative way of combining the two, especially as some of the larger in-theatre catering outlets have training opportunities. In other words, consider applying your catering skills to theatre. You will meet actors, technicians and creatives, and have a chance to see the shows at some sort of concessionary rate, if not free.

In 2012, *The Stage* announced three Unsung Hero Awards as part of its annual Stage 100 Awards – someone who has contributed to an organisation's ongoing success but whose effort might otherwise be unnoticed. One of these went to Frances Coyle, manager of the coffee bar at Glasgow Citizens Theatre. *The Stage*'s tribute to her said:

> Glasgow's Citizens Theatre has benefited from the service of Frances Coyle for more than forty years. She joined the venue in 1967 and is only just retiring now from her position in the theatre's coffee bar, aged eighty-two. Coyle was nominated by the Head of Operations at the Citizens Theatre, Lesley Davidson. Speaking as

Coyle's line manager for the past eleven years, Davidson said Coyle had worked 'tirelessly' and that she 'can still out-work the young ones'. In her nomination, Davidson added: 'To my knowledge, she has never taken a sick day and has only been off when she had one of her many children way back in the fifties and sixties.' Of Coyle's eight children, two have worked at the Citz alongside their mother, and Coyle's granddaughter is currently on the staff at the theatre, meaning that three generations of the family have all supported the venue. The judges felt Coyle's service perfectly encapsulated the spirit of the new Unsung Hero Award and her dedication to the Citizens over the past forty years struck us as outstanding.

This all goes to prove that catering work is a very worthwhile way of working in theatre!

Useful websites

Theatre Royal, Bury St Edmunds www.theatreroyal.org

York Theatre Royal www.yorktheatreroyal.co.uk

Publicity

What do publicity staff do?

All theatres and shows have to be marketed to ensure an audience and income. If it's a very small fringe show that may mean printing some posters and flyers and putting them up around the local community. In a very small company, there may be a single admin person for whom marketing and publicity is just one small part of what he or she does. At the other end of the scale, big companies have departments with several staff responsible for making sure that the world knows as much as possible about the organisation's work.

Titles and roles in publicity include:

- Head/Director of Publicity/Communications
- Press Officer (or assistant/administrator/manager)
- Communications Assistant (or officer/manager/ assistant)
- Marketing Manager (or assistant/administrator/ officer)

And, in large companies, many of these jobs will have sub-divisions and/or deputy posts as well.

Some press officers have worked as journalists. Others have studied public relations or marketing at university, or done other training in it after a degree in something else. But many just start in a marketing department, perhaps in a junior administrative post or some sort of placement or internship and simply work their way up.

They prepare press releases to send to journalists, and the good ones build up a good working relationship with the journalists they deal with regularly to ensure the best possible press coverage for their company.

Sarah Munday is the Press Officer at Marlowe Theatre, Canterbury. Now in a brand-new building, it was closed for redevelopment for two-and-a-half years until it reopened in 2011.

'I am a journalist by profession, with seventeen years' experience in local newspapers – National Council of Journalism Training (NCJT) trained and qualified. I started as a trainee reporter and ended up in the same office working as acting editor/news editor with three weekly titles and a team of ten to deal with! I came to a point where I decided I'd had enough. I went for a job as a police press officer – but thankfully didn't get it, because I then applied for the Marlowe job. I already had a love of theatre (and in particular, dance) and was a regular at the theatre as a reviewer which, of course, helped.

My job is to promote the Marlowe and its activities – not all show-related – to local, regional and national media. I write press releases, deal with press enquiries, organise and manage interviews and photocalls, and write and edit the Marlowe Friends magazine, as well as articles for other publications. I also organise and manage press nights and promotional events.

No two days are the same. One day might be taken up with a press launch, which I will organise. Another day I might be reading a proof of the new Friends magazine. Typical days will include dealing with lots of emails, a meeting or two, phone calls and the odd visit backstage or elsewhere in the theatre to talk to someone about press coverage.

Anyone wanting to do this job needs writing ability, good social skills and a genuine love and understanding of theatre. And it's very important to be "up" on all the new social media, like Twitter and Facebook.'

How do you become a theatre publicist?

Get yourself educated in public relations, media or journalism – probably at university. And, as with so much theatre work, see as many shows as you can in different venues so that you have some sense of what theatres produce.

Then look for advertised posts. These days you may have to start with an unpaid or expenses-only internship. Regard it as your opportunity to learn from others and hone your skills. If you can prove you can do the job, then you are well placed to apply for a similar paid post – either in the same venue or elsewhere.

OTHER JOBS

It is inevitable in a book of this sort that many jobs in theatre have defied my attempts to categorise them, and so we end up with at least one miscellany chapter – the jobs that got away.

Agents, education staff, critics and other writers, including those who create programme notes, are an important part of the theatre industry.

So are chaperones for the many children who perform in professional shows and the highly skilled people who make theatre accessible to audience members with impairments.

Also in this chapter, I've included stage-door staff – an important reception and administrative role.

- EDUCATION OFFICER   114
- WRITER   121
- AGENT   129
- CHAPERONE   134
- INTERPRETER   137
- STAGE-DOOR STAFF   142

Education Officer

Most theatres and theatre companies are involved, to some degree, in education. It can be something as simple as offering show-related activity packs and basic opportunities to question the cast after a performance of a show. At the other end of the spectrum, education work can involve large-scale sponsored projects which involve hundreds of young people in creating their own work in response to shows. To do that, companies employ facilitators who go into schools to run workshops and support teachers in developing young people's skills.

A big company, such as the RSC for instance, has a large education department. Jacqui O'Hanlon, Director of Education, is regarded as an important section head within the company – which overall employs six to seven hundred people at any one time, including actors, permanent or casual members of staff and freelances. Of these, a number well into double figures will be in the education department, which runs teacher training in partnership with the University of Warwick, ongoing actor training – especially in helping actors to learn facilitation skills – and many projects within schools.

Education is not, of course, limited to children, young people and schools. Theatre companies and venues also work with vulnerable adults, specific groups such as refugees, ex-offenders, or Bengali women – just to cite three at random – or large sections of the population such as over-sixties. Some activities are simply laid on for, and open to, anyone who's interested.

People involved in theatre-related education work come with various titles, including Education Office/Manager/Facilitator and Programme Administrator/Leader. Head or Director of Learning is another common one.

In a small company, the education officer may be part-time – perhaps doing a similar job in more than one theatre – or do the education work as part of a larger brief for a single company.

It is a field of the theatre industry that has grown enormously in recent years. As one education officer remarked to me recently, 'Thirty years ago you could have held a meeting of all theatre-based education staff and got them into one small room. Now you'd need the Royal Albert Hall.'

What does an education officer do?

The work is very varied and depends – obviously – on the exact nature of your job. You might be a facilitator leading a project out in schools, probably on a freelance basis – almost as if you were a teacher. You could be mainly office-based, planning and organising events and/or trying to raise funds to pay for them. Or you could, like Jacqui O'Hanlon, be directing a large number of staff while still having a hand in projects at ground level and liaising with senior staff in the rest of the company.

Charlie Payne is the Almeida Theatre's Schools and Education Manager.

'My role is largely office-based, and focuses on the work we do with education groups and schools (including teachers). I don't usually deliver on projects personally – aside from backstage tours and an occasional Q&A. So much of my role is coordination, sat at the computer, managing schedules, booking staff and, until recently, managing the schools booking system, including booking workshops. I also write the education resource packs for our shows. It's a really varied role and no two days are the same. Generally every day involves responding to questions via email – whether from teachers who want tickets or a workshop, or facilitators checking details for where they're working, or people sending in CVs, as well as the more general enquiries about what we do. Then there are the other, more specific tasks. Today, for example, I'm doing some research into the A level English Literature syllabus for the resource pack accompanying the theatre's production of *King Lear*. This afternoon I will be firming up the schedule for our autumn (and spring) schools residency projects and checking dates when the theatre's free before formalising my proposal to take to schools – I'll be out and about having meetings with them in the coming weeks. When a project's up and running, I'll work with the administrative assistant to ensure our staff and school contracts are returned, session plans and evaluations are sent in and are shipshape, and generally ensuring that all on the residency are happy with the ongoing work.'

How do you become an education officer?

Some are former teachers, usually with a major interest in drama. Jobs labelled 'primary- or secondary-school teaching experience would be an advantage' sometimes appear in the education press and/or the performing-arts press and relevant websites.

Others are former actors who do some education work on the side and decide that they prefer it to being on stage –

and so become specialists. Or they volunteer to lead show-related education workshops and other sessions because it's another source of income. Many people who work in theatre are 'portfolio people', doing several different jobs at the same time.

Some in-theatre education staff have been administrators in a theatre or elsewhere. Gradually, as the potential for education has grown, education has become part – or sometimes all – of what they do.

In most cases, education staff bring other skills to the job but learn what in-theatre education means as they go along. But because the field has grown so much in recent years, many drama schools (Royal Central School of Speech and Drama, East 15 and Birmingham School of Acting, for example) and universities (such as Manchester and Exeter) now run drama courses focused on applied theatre and/or education. These courses typically give the students lots of project experience and are a pretty sound basis for anyone drawn to an education role in theatre.

'I did a degree in Drama at the University of Manchester. It was quite an academic course rather than practical, which taught us widely about theatre practitioners, including Augusto Boal, and applied-theatre theory. I wrote my dissertation on theatre activity following the ACE's Theatre Policy 2000 and the Boyden Report, both of which set out the importance of education in theatres. I spoke to a number of Manchester theatres' artistic directors, and they all stressed the importance of this. I was also involved in some outreach work (as a participant) with Open Contact at the Contact Theatre. After uni, I moved back home to Hampshire and got a 'proper job' (i.e. temping/working in an office, very dull), and saved up for a year away. Then I landed an apprenticeship in Administration and Development at the Donmar Warehouse in London, where I stayed for three months, all the time applying for jobs, going to interviews, not to mention lapping up every opportunity to learn about the industry in real time from the people around me at the Donmar. It wasn't paid, and it was a tough three months – the extortionate Hampshire–London train fare (back then about £350 a month, for a 16–25 railcard holder!), not to mention the lunch expenses, being based in Covent Garden. I'd go home from the internship and work in pubs and a club over the weekend. Those were long, long days, but it was worth it. The internship meant I was getting lots of interviews, nearly all for entry-level jobs, in general admin and marketing. Finally I got a job at the Orange Tree Theatre (OTT) – its crazy job title was "Office Manager/ Education Officer/PA to the Directors". Yes! All three!

I remember talking in my interview about how passionate I was about theatre education, and how important it had been. I'd had so little in my state education in Hampshire, but the experiences I'd had in an actual theatre had left a lasting impression. At the OTT I worked closely on the schools programme, which ranged from primary to secondary and included productions for young people. I realised that the education side was something I was keen to pursue in more depth, and the job at the OTT didn't leave much time to focus on that – on top of changing printer cartridges and ordering stationery for the whole office! So I applied for – and got – a job at the Almeida Theatre, as administrator for Almeida Projects, the education department, where I was to be based full time in the thick of the theatre's work with

> young people and the community. I've been there for over five years now and my job has developed immensely – from basic admin to helping produce our productions for young people and project-managing our residencies with local schools. It's really satisfying because you see the results up close, you see the impact on young people who maybe are visiting the theatre for the first time, and you realise that's what it's all about, really!'
>
> *Charlie Payne*

If you really want to work in a theatre's education department, the best advice is probably to get out there and do it. Experience is what will make you stand out and it doesn't have to be professional, or acting, either. Anything that proves you have an active interest in working in theatre education – in any way – is to your credit. So if you're still at school, college, or in a job you'd like to escape from, try volunteering at your local youth theatre or youth club.

Yes, you'll need a relevant degree, but there are many more graduates now than there once were and experience on your CV will help to distinguish you. An internship, like the one Charlie Payne did, is a very good route in, if you can afford it (cheaper than a postgraduate course, though), and gives you direct, on-the-job learning experience.

Or you might take part in schemes, such as the Young Friends of the Almeida, which offer more than just 'acting' and include learning about the industry. There are similar schemes at the Lyric Hammersmith and Ovalhouse in London. And most regional theatres offer some way for young people to engage with them. Most of this activity is subsidised (or free) so it needn't leave you out of pocket. If you don't see anything on a company's website, then ask – the worst they can say is 'no', and the best you've done is show willing. Being proactive is very important.

Useful websites

Almeida Theatre (Education Department)
www.almeida.co.uk/education

RSC (Education Department) www.rsc.org.uk/education

Writer

Playwrights, as we have seen, write plays – but what about people who write, in various ways, about theatre rather than directly for it?

Theatre writers include:

- Critics who review plays and other performances for newspapers, magazines and websites.

- Arts journalists who report on theatre-related news.

- Writers of informative essays or interviews in theatre programmes.

- Biographers who write the life stories of actors and other theatre practitioners.

- People who write education packs and other show-linked materials to help teachers wanting to use a piece of theatre as part of their students' learning.

- Writers of copy for companies' websites. In the case of a small company it is probably just part of the work of someone with a different job in the company. Big organisations, such as the RSC and the Royal Opera House, employ or hire freelance writers.

Some critics – such as Michael Billington of the *Guardian* and Charles Spencer of the *Daily Telegraph* – become very well known because they have been doing the job for many years and everything they write is based on enormous experience. Critics at this level have usually started with a degree, often in English, at a good university, before starting work as a junior journalist who gradually becomes a theatre specialist. Billington and Spencer, for example, both went to the University of Oxford.

No one can teach you how to review. You learn by doing it and, in general, the longer you've been doing it, the better you will be.

In practice, most critics also write other things – such as programme essays, biographies or other books – as well. In 2008, Michael Billington won the annual Society for Theatre Research Award for his book *State of the Nation: British Theatre Since 1945*. He has also written books about Peggy Ashcroft, Tom Stoppard and Alan Ayckbourn and is the official, authorised biographer of Harold Pinter.

Mark Shenton, who reviews for *The Stage* and *Sunday Express*, also does other forms of journalism such as interviews. He writes a daily blog for *The Stage* website too and sometimes writes informative background pieces for theatre programmes.

Or take me. I do a fair bit of reviewing, particularly of shows for young audiences, but I write plenty of other things as well. I do general journalism in *The Stage* and elsewhere – and I'm writing this book.

There is probably no such thing as a full-time critic.

What does a theatre writer do?

He or she sees a lot of theatre – usually using complimentary tickets (given by press or publicity people working for the production company) to writers (who need information and are likely to help publicise the show).

Over time, the writer builds up contacts. Press officers and people in charge of marketing a show become regular ports of call. They will often offer the writer interviews with directors, actors, playwrights and so on. And anyone who wants to interview actors has to make a point of 'knowing' the main agents who represent them. Eventually, the writer has a strong 'contacts book' – which may, these days, be a computer file or email address book – and can get in touch with helpful people quite easily.

A theatre writer probably spends as much time networking and researching – which includes seeing shows – as he or she does actually sitting down to write. And keeping the two things in balance – as I know from personal experience – is an ongoing struggle.

Some theatre writers are staff journalists on newspapers. Quentin Letts, for example, is employed by the *Daily Mail*, for which he also writes material which is not related to theatre.

Many more are freelance, sometimes with part-time contracts which tie their reviews and columns to a single outlet and an agreement not to write for competing titles. But that doesn't prevent them from writing other material for other publications, or from writing books, programme notes and so on. There are, in fact, ever fewer staff jobs in the media and an increasing number of journalists who would once have been employed are now freelance.

Not that writing about theatre begins and ends with journalism. Helen Cadbury writes show-related education packs and teaching materials for drama educators and teachers through her company, TheatreStudy.

TheatreStudy Education Packs are created by Helen Cadbury, a specialist in drama education since 1989.

Helen trained as an actor and performed in national touring, young people's theatre and TIE companies. She subsequently became a teacher and has taught at primary, secondary and post-sixteen level, and in youth-arts and youth-theatre settings.

> She was Education Director for Schools at York The-
> atre Royal, Consultant Education Director for Compass
> Theatre Company and is currently an Education Asso-
> ciate for Pilot Theatre and a visiting lecturer at Royal
> Central School of Speech and Drama.
>
> 'Additional material is researched and written by prac-
> tising teachers and theatre professionals and
> resources packs are "test driven" in real learning envi-
> ronments.'
>
> *From the TheatreStudy website*

Writing is a very adaptable skill. If you can write in one way, you can probably quite easily train yourself to write in another. Someone who is used to writing for newspapers and magazines can readily adjust to producing online copy. Biographers can usually produce articles if required. An interview or essay in a programme is really just another form of article.

How do you become a theatre writer?

The best starting point is an obvious one: see as much theatre as you can so that you've got something to write about.

Writing skills are developed in two main ways. First, you need to read a lot in the genre in which you need to write. So read reviews, interviews with theatre people, theatrical biographies, programme notes and even education packs (which are often available to download free from a company's website).

An interesting and useful self-training exercise is to see a major show which will be widely reviewed. Before you read anything about it, have a go at reviewing it yourself, then read as many professional reviews as you can. Compare your reaction with what the experts say and – most importantly – study the way that top-notch reviews are constructed. Note, for example, that words are never wasted. The writing is always 'tight', and adjectives such as 'marvellous' or 'dreadful' are generally not used because they are vague. Vocabulary has to be very specific.

Second, writing is like swimming, driving or reading: you can be instructed and given tips but you actually learn all these things by doing them. And you learn to write by writing. So if you want to be a theatre writer, you should be writing as much as possible.

Nobody in the twenty-first century, incidentally, will care whether you've been to Oxbridge or not. If you can write well people will want to read what you've written. For example, neither Caitlin Moran (*The Times*) nor Bryony Gordon (*Daily Telegraph*) – both youngish, highly successful writers – went to university at all.

If you're still at school, college or university, hone your skills by writing about in-house and local theatre for student magazines and websites.

It is very easy, and cheap, to set up your own blog. Start one for your theatre writing – reviews, musings, observations and interviews if you can get them. Publicise it through social-networking sites such as Facebook, Twitter and LinkedIn. It's excellent practice and, if your work is good, there is always a chance that your efforts will be noticed by a commercial publisher.

Once you have developed some real writing skill, offer to write for websites such as A Younger Theatre, Stage Won or Sardines Magazine. You won't be paid but each of these has a sizeable readership and it will help to put you and your name on the map. It also gives you credibility – if you have a commission from one of these (and there are other equally respected theatre websites), you will be taken seriously when you approach companies and their PR people for free tickets.

Keep a cuttings folder – in hard copy or online – and maintain an up-to-date CV which highlights your theatre -writing skills.

Look for internships in theatre companies or in the media which will involve writing.

Consider training as a journalist on a course accredited by the National Council of Journalism Training (NCJT) – typically a postgraduate year in a college or university, but bear in mind that there are lot of people succeeding in the world of theatre writing who have never done any specific journalism or other writing training.

The time-honoured way of getting a toe in the door is to write something catchy and original and to send it to a newspaper section editor who, if you're very lucky, might publish it. That's what I did (*TES* and then the *Daily Telegraph*) back in 1990. There are fewer opportunities today because newspapers and their budgets have shrunk – but it is probably still worth trying.

Look very carefully at the publication you're aiming at, though. Find a slot that appears to be written by a different person every day or week, and style your piece accordingly. Consider slots in local papers too – they are, obviously, easier to get into because there's much less competition.

There is no single route into writing – almost every theatre writer you speak to will tell you a different story. If and when you meet practitioners at networking events, it's worth asking the question, 'How did you get to be a theatre writer?' for that very reason.

Heather Neill was arts editor at the TES *for many years. Today she is a freelance theatre writer.*

'I began by writing a specimen review which I sent in to the *TES*, not for publication, but in the hope of getting some writing work. I was a teacher and had directed a few productions. As a student I'd read English, done some drama – including reviewing – at university and spent most of my vacations selling programmes at the National Theatre. The Arts Editor, Michael Church, was new to the job and thought I'd be a useful recruit, so I began by reviewing school plays and theatre-in-education productions. After a year of freelancing for the *TES*, I was invited to apply for a job as a subeditor on the paper. I got the job and continued to write about theatre whenever possible.

After two or three years, I took over from Helen Dawson, the journalist who had been writing and editing National Theatre programmes. I used to dash to the British Museum Reading Room in my lunch hour, order books one day and work on them the next. I kept up this regime for about a year but it became untenable. Many years later, however, I still write pieces for NT programmes, now edited by Lyn Haill, who was already on the staff when I started.

After a few years, I began freelancing for *The Times* and then other broadsheets, interviewing actors, directors and playwrights, and writing features on theatre subjects. Most newspapers would not allow staff members to write for other national publications, but the *TES* didn't have a direct rival – although I was discouraged from contributing to the *Guardian* as it carried a significant range of educational advertising. I eventually became Deputy Arts and Literary Editor and then Arts and Literary Editor at *TES*. I have been freelance since 2003.

As a freelance, my situation is unusual in that I often work directly for theatres. Although I do some reviewing, I am not attached to a particular publication. I wrote about Globe Education for the *TES* long before the theatre itself was built. I was asked to be a member of the education advisory committee and then to chair the publications committee there. Nowadays I contribute to Globe programmes and *Around the Globe* magazine, and I chair events and lead discussions in summer schools. I have also contributed to WhatsOnStage.com and often interview for the radio website TheatreVOICE.

There is no such thing as a "normal" day for a freelance. Most days involve some contact with editors or theatre people in order to set up or deliver work. Networking is important; one thing sometimes leads to another. You need to be flexible and willing to respond quickly.

When I started, hardly anyone trained to be a journalist. Now most do. Take a course if you can, but energy and enthusiasm and then experience will get you further than anything. Remember you too are part of showbiz and you will probably have to "sell" what you can do in a very overcrowded profession. You have to be a fearless, enthusiastic communicator.'

Useful websites

Stage Won www.stagewon.co.uk

Sardines Magazine www.sardinesmagazine.co.uk

TheatreStudy www.theatrestudy.co.uk

TheatreVOICE www.theatrevoice.com

A Younger Theatre www.ayoungertheatre.com

Agent

Agents are paid a percentage of earnings by actors to help find them work. An actor is taken on to agency books – a contract. The agent or agency then promotes the actor and suggests him or her for suitable roles as and when they come up.

In practice, finding a suitable agent is one of the biggest hurdles for an actor who is finishing training and ready to seek professional work. Agents attend student shows and showcases and approach the students they are interested in. Some very talented and promising young actors will have many agents competing to represent them. Others struggle to find anyone to represent them months or even years after the completion of their training.

Agents are steeped in theatre and the workings of the theatre industry. They know exactly who is casting what, when and where, and who might be suitable for which role.

Some agents work as individuals. Most work in groups – agencies – although an actor is usually assigned to a specific individual in the company who 'looks after' him or her.

Some agencies deal only with actors and other performers. Others also have departments for writers and others needing representation in order to secure freelance work.

What does an agent do?

He or she liaises between actors they represent and casting directors. The whole object is to ensure that actors secure the best and most suitable roles and then arrange the most advantageous possible contract and payment.

Good agents have an immensely detailed knowledge and understanding of the industry, and large numbers of contacts within it. This takes many years to build up but there are ways in at the bottom.

James Foster, twenty-six, is a Junior Agent at Jeremy Brook Limited, which represents about sixty actors. Foster and Brook manage the load between them.

'No two days in the office are the same. We have clients at all career stages so the day is very varied. Each day we work on breakdowns of TV/film/theatre/commercials/radio/corporate work that comes in and suggest our actors accordingly.

We give out appointments (audition meetings) to the clients and ensure they are well briefed for their meetings with directors/casting directors so that they go fully informed.

We sometimes get calls from casting directors who aren't one hundred per cent sure of what/who they are looking for. They will pick our brains and we're able to say, "How about so-and-so?", etc.

We advise our clients on their potential. Sometimes someone thinks he is Romeo when in actual fact he's more of a Mercutio. It's about having a dialogue and being absolutely honest and realistic but sensitive.

Our working day doesn't finish at 6 p.m. Not only do we have to see the shows our clients are in, we are also inundated with invitations to various shows ranging from press nights and drama-school shows, to fringe shows and shows in the regions. Whilst we can't cover everything, we do make an effort to go whenever possible.'

An agent has to be very confident in manner. He or she spends a lot of time talking on the phone. You need to be able to communicate both with actors and casting directors in a clear and honest way.

How do you become an agent?

Although many of the seasoned, well-known agents who've been working in the industry for many years are not graduates, today most newcomers to the profession will have been to university or, perhaps, drama school.

If you want to work as an agent in theatre, you need to know as much as you can about plays – so choose a degree course that gives you the opportunity to see, read and study as many plays of as possible. Drama is an obvious choice, and so is English. While you are at university, go and see as many plays as you can – from a very low-budget, one-person fringe show in the back room of a pub and anything produced by fellow students, to large-scale subsidised work. There are almost always schemes to keep ticket costs down for students.

Then try writing to some agents who look for internships. Some offices will accept work-experience students. Be clear – both to yourself and others – about why you want to become an agent. Forget glamour and parties. It's hard work and a great responsibility. You need to love theatre, television and films, because you'll spend a lot of time watching them.

'I was very lucky in how I came to be a junior agent. Having initially trained as an actor, I worked for a year performing in plays such as *'Tis Pity She's a Whore* and *She Stoops to Conquer*. I ended up working back as an administrative assistant at my old drama school, Italia Conti. Then I was recommended to Jeremy Brook as an assistant because he was looking for someone one day a week. As time went on I was struck by the agent bug and wanted to do it more, so one day became two, became three and eventually full-time.

After a year, I was promoted to Junior Agent as opposed to assistant. That was surprisingly fast, but I think Jeremy was prepared to take a risk because he knew I knew my stuff. For three years at drama school I was never out of the theatre. I saw something like five hundred or more plays and worked on a number during my training. I had always read not just plays but literature around the subject, such as drama theory or biographies. I made it my job to be informed and to know what was going on, who was directing what, who was casting what, where my favourite actors were appearing and so on. I really made sure I was a sponge and I worked hard to be informed about the industry I was going into.

Working as an agent is not something you can train for specifically, but you can prepare yourself from your teens by reading and watching. Know Shakespeare, know Wilde, Shaw and Ibsen, know Ravenhill, Butterworth and Polly Stenham. Know what's hot now and what was hot then. Working as an agent, you never know what play is going to be revived or what piece of new writing is going to come out, but anyone who is well read is well informed. Go to the theatre. Watch your favourite actors. Watch shows you know you might not like but that you can learn from. Watch classic films as well as new ones. Don't ever limit yourself but strive to know more than the next person.

I was able to talk about why I liked a playwright, why I didn't like a piece of theatre, why I didn't like an actor in a particular TV series. It's not about being negative or arrogant, but it's about being able to have an opinion on the world you work or would like to work in.'

James Foster

Chaperone

What does a chaperone do?

She or he accompanies children to work in the theatre and acts as a buffer between the boy or girl performer and the show's directors, cast and creators. The main purpose of a chaperone is to protect the child from exploitation – such as being asked to work more than the licensed hours or to do something arguably dangerous on stage which has not been previously agreed and assessed for risk.

In practice, especially in the case of a show that is not touring, the child's own parent will often act as chaperone. Whether the chaperone is a parent or a paid professional, he or she has to be with the child at all times – except on stage, obviously,

When a show – *Oliver!*, for example, using a large cast of children – is touring, some of the children in the main roles will travel with it. They stay in carefully managed accommodation where they are looked after by chaperones who become temporary substitute parents, rather like staff in the boarding houses of residential schools.

A chaperone can look after more than one child. Sometimes it's a group.

Heather Miller has been a leading theatre chaperone for more than twenty years, and winner of one of the three 2012 Stage 100 Unsung Hero Awards.

'We are currently touring with *Oliver!* My team and I are looking after twenty-four boys aged between eight and fourteen. Of these, twelve tour with us. The others are recruited locally. I wake them in the morning, run their baths, get them to breakfast and then to school on time. I also have to establish a trusting relationship with their main carers – usually mums and dads – and tell them what we're doing on a daily basis.'

How do you become a chaperone?

The first step is to get DBS (Disclosure and Barring Service) clearance – for which you will have to pay. You have to be able, for obvious reasons, to demonstrate that you have no history or convictions for any sort of child abuse. Even parents chaperoning their own children usually have to do this because they might find themselves also chaperoning, or with access to, other people's children. Getting this clearance can also involve an interview. More information about how to go about this is available via the Home Office website (www.homeoffice.gov.uk/agencies-public-bodies/dbs).

You need to be very fond of children and to be able to act as a parent for a child who is not your own. That means being kind, patient and sympathetic, as well as firm and authoritative.

Most professional chaperones start by chaperoning their own children, realise that they like it, and gradually move into it as a paid job.

Heather Miller, for instance, chaperoned her own daughter before a change in family circumstances forced her to become the breadwinner. She was offered a paid job on a Christmas/New Year show by someone who had seen her in operation and liked her approach. It was the break she needed to launch her career.

There are, it has to be said, few openings, because jobs tend to be assigned via an informal network of casting directors, producers, agents and known reliable chaperones.

> 'Wherever we go on tour there are usually local chaperones whom we know and trust because we've worked with them before, and they tend to be the ones we employ. But we do take on new people too. For example, we've just given a year's contract to a young woman of twenty-two in Cardiff who is very good with children and keen on theatre.'
>
> *Heather Miller*

Chaperones need to know and understand the many regulations that affect both their own dealings with the children in their charge and the ones affecting what the children may or may not do in the show.

Liking theatre is really secondary to all this, although Heather Miller, who is very self-effacing and certainly would never have wanted to perform, says she has gradually grown to love theatre over the years.

Sometimes big tours advertise in *The Stage* for chaperones. It could also be worth approaching theatrical agencies which have children on their books because they may well deal with chaperones too.

Chaperones in TV and film are usually better paid than their counterparts in theatre, but you can expect at least the BECTU (Broadcasting, Entertainment, Cinematograph and Theatre Union) minimum rate for backstage work. It is the company which pays chaperones, and is, for them, an unavoidable overhead incurred by employing child performers.

Interpreter

In recent years, the theatre industry has become commendably proactive about finding imaginative ways of making theatre as accessible as possible to audience members who have sight or hearing impairments.

Regular theatregoers have, for instance, become used to the presence, for certain performances, of an interpreter at the side of the playing area translating the text, as the actors speak it, into British Sign Language.

Most theatres offer a loop system for people who need to hear the play at a higher volume and some performances are captioned.

Less well known, to people who don't need them at least, are pre-show set tours for blind people. Invited to arrive early at the theatre, people with impaired sight are taken onto the set, and meet some of the cast in costume. They can touch the set and the costumes, which are also described for them, so that they have an appreciation of what other people are seeing during the play.

In some theatres for some performances, blind people can also opt to hear an audio description, which is a live commentary on the action, not unlike a very sympathetic sports commentary on radio. The describer describes the set, explains what the actors are doing, and tells his or her listeners what is happening on stage, including comments on things like lighting and special effects. All this is spoken in the spaces when actors aren't speaking and the user, sitting in the audience, hears it via headphones.

What does an interpreter do?

Interpreters have very specific skills and specialisms and have often undergone long training. It takes about seven years to master British Sign Language at the required level, for example.

Interpreters are almost always freelance and most work only part-time as theatre interpreters.

Sometimes interpreters also work front of house to meet and greet theatregoers with impairments, help them to their seats and so on.

An interpreter employed to 'sign' a performance must have some theatrical knowledge and appreciation. She or he should get the script about four weeks beforehand, depending on the time allocated for rehearsal. The interpreter also needs to be fully au fait with staging, entrances and exits – which means attending some rehearsals. In practice, the interpreter has to know the script – every part – almost as well as the actors do because the interpretation has to be simultaneous, very slick and totally accurate.

'English humour is particularly difficult to interpret,' said Sula Gleeson, vice-chair of Signed Performance in Theatre (SPIT) and herself an interpreter.

It is very hard work physically. Most actors leave the stage for part of the performance in most shows. But the interpreter 'performs' continuously on his or her feet throughout the show, which can be three hours or more if, say, it's a full-length Shakespeare play. Most signers registered with SPIT do not do more than about six shows a year so they need other work as well.

Theatre companies such as Graeae, which specialise in work for disabled people, have a team of interpreters they work with regularly and, inevitably, there is an informal network of interpreters.

Fees for British Sign Language interpreting work vary. The best rates, not unexpectedly, are in London.

Audio description is slightly less technical because the describer doesn't have to learn a new language. Like the BSL interpreter, though, the describer needs to be totally familiar with what is happening and being said in the play. That means advance studying of the script and attending some performances. He or she also needs to be very fluent and to have a well-modulated voice.

The interpreter is then present in the theatre describing the show. In many cases, he or she is also involved in touch tours and/or may have pre-recorded an introduction for the blind or partially sighted person to listen to in advance.

VocalEyes is a nationwide audio-description charity. It provides access to the arts for blind and partially sighted people, and aims for them to share the experience with their friends and family. Their live description of a theatre production (drama, comedy, musical, opera, circus, ballet or contemporary dance) contains three essential elements:

- Describing the key visual elements of the show.

- Pre-show audio introductory notes on CD or as an MP3 download from the website.

- A touch-tour of set and stage.

How do you become an interpreter?

There is, as yet, no clear 'professional status' career path for interpreters, according to Sula Gleeson, who says that the situation is constantly changing. SPIT wants to raise the standards of interpretation.

The National Register of Communication Professionals working with Deaf and Deafblind People (NRCPD) lists approved, qualified practitioners.

Meanwhile, Gleeson suggests that you consider a degree in BSL (such as the ones offered by University of Central Lancashire and Heriot Watt University in Edinburgh) which is a Level 6 qualification. There are also graded BSL courses in further-education colleges.

You can then work in courts, for the police and in medical settings as well, which you will need to do because there is not a great deal of work in theatre. Some theatres run no signed performances at all because they are too expensive to mount and it isn't always possible to find a sponsor.

There is no central register of specialist theatre interpreters, although SPIT is slowly working towards creating one.

Anyone wanting to work in theatre as an interpreter – either in signing or description – needs to be passionate about theatre, with a lot of knowledge about plays and how they work. That is probably partly why some actors train to be interpreters as a second string to their professional bow.

The Royal National Institute for the Blind (RNIB) recommends the training offered by the Audio Description Association (ADA) and Audio Description Association Scotland (ADAS). Their courses are accredited by Open College Network at Level 3. It gives you a Certificate in Audio Description Skills which is the nationally recognised qualification for describers in the UK.

Another training option is to do either the MA in Monolingual Subtitling and Audio Description at the University of Surrey or the one in Audiovisual Translation at Roehampton University.

VocalEyes offers training too. Its tutors include professional broadcasters, performers and published authors. The training can be pitched at any level according to the needs of the trainees, who can be beginners or established practitioners.

Describers can be professionals or volunteers. As with so many aspects of in-theatre work, beginning as an enthusiastic, utterly reliable volunteer – and seeing where it takes you – is probably a good way in.

Useful websites

ADA www.audiodescription.co.uk

ADAS www.adascotland.com

NRCPD www.nrcpd.org.uk

RNIB www.rnib.org.uk

SPIT www.spit.org.uk

VocalEyes www.vocaleyes.co.uk

Stage-door Staff

The stage door is the staff entrance to the theatre. Actors, technicians, stage managers, administrators and anyone else who works in the building enters via the stage door, which is usually hidden away at the back or side of the theatre.

What do stage-door staff do?

The door has to be continually staffed when the theatre is open – typically from 9.00 or 10.00 in the morning if there are rehearsals or other events, until late at night after the show has 'come down' (ended) and everyone has gone home. That means that stage-door staff usually work shifts.

The job includes reception duties – seeing people in and out, answering queries and dealing with visitors. There is also a security element. The staff are, quite literally, 'door-keepers', ensuring that no one gets into the theatre who shouldn't. That is probably partly why the stage-door entrance is often quite narrow and the vestibule small so that it can be supervised quite easily by one or two people.

Linda Tolhurst has been stage-door supervisor at the National Theatre for seventeen years, and worked at the National Theatre doing office work and occasional shifts covering the stage door before that.

'The NT stage door is a bit different from many (but not all) stage doors because we are also the reception

and switchboard for the administration side of the theatre. A typical day is split into two halves – day and evening. The day is primarily concerned with the admin side of the theatre, taking calls, dealing with visitors, couriers, contacting casting if there are auditions. Most of it is like reception work anywhere else, except for matinee days when you would be giving actors their post/messages, and the first day of rehearsals when you are the first point of contact for new company members.

The evening is primarily concerned with the artistic side of the theatre, so you would again be giving company members their post/messages, calling cabs and dealing with their visitors after the performance. We do the same for technical and creative staff as well.

If you want a job like mine, sadly there is no Stage Door School. So my advice to anyone wanting to get into this line of work would be (and I know this may sound strange) to be up to date with what's on in TV, films and theatre. It really does help if you recognise someone from TV or whatever who has just walked into your stage door – and it can sometimes give both them and you a buzz.'

How do you become stage-door staff?

Computer skills are a must nowadays, as most switchboards are computerised and also act as your PC. A good memory helps when someone comes through the stage door who may have been there previously for a show, just to visit, or has been in for an audition. Two of the main qualities you need are the senses: common and humour.

Finally, a way in is if you live near a theatre, visit its stage door and ask if you could possibly spend a day/evening with staff just to get a feeling for what goes on. You could also try front-of-house work and offer your services to the stage door. Once you have a foot in the door, a whole range of opportunities can be open to you. Don't be afraid to give it a go because it can be very rewarding.

Further reading for other theatre jobs

Drama Games for Classrooms and Workshops, Jessica Swale (Nick Hern Books, 2009)

Kenneth Tynan: Theatre Writings, ed. Dominic Shellard (Nick Hern Books, 2008)

State of the Nation: British Theatre Since 1945, Michael Billington (Faber, 2007)

Theatre and Education, Helen Nicholson (Palgrave Macmillan, 2009)

Theatre, Education and Performance, Helen Nicholson (Palgrave Macmillan, 2011)

Part Three

Acting – If You Really Must

I have, in this book so far, quite deliberately played down the possibility of working in theatre as a performer.

I wanted, first, to make the reader fully aware of the enormous range of job opportunities there are in theatre apart from the tiny, obvious ones you see on stage when you buy a ticket and sit in the audience.

And it is the backstage and 'beyond stage' jobs that careers advisers and teachers are not, on the whole, telling young people about.

Nonetheless, every show does need performers. And there will always be people who are, despite the hurdles and challenges, absolutely determined to pursue an onstage career.

Here I shall often use the word 'actor'. Many female actors now dislike the term 'actress' so I've plumped for the generic 'actor' to include both sexes.

These days there's a great deal more to acting than, well, acting.

All actors are, at times, expected to sing, and dance. Circus skills, puppetry and other accomplishments are often required in shows today. Many actors also play musical instruments and there are several training courses specifically to develop the skills of actor-musicians.

For many years now, musical theatre has been growing faster than any other sector in the industry – to such an extent that some critics and commentators have expressed concern that in London's West End, at least, there are now too few 'straight' plays because musical theatre dominates.

All theatre needs versatility. But performers in musical theatre need to be equally skilled in acting, singing and dancing: the so called 'triple-threat performer'.

Kenneth Avery-Clark, Principal and Head of Voice at London's American Musical Theatre Academy (AMTA), has appeared in the West End in Sweet Charity, The Drowsy Chaperone, The Producers, Ragtime *and* 125th Street.

'There isn't a single dancer working on the West End stage today. Even someone who trained primarily as a dancer now has to perform in other ways as well. You don't train to be a dancer any more. You train to be a performer.'

What does – or can – an actor do?

Well, the most obvious and visible thing an actor does is to play roles on stage (or screen) in front of an audience. That can mean appearing in eight shows a week – six evenings and two matinees. But, as with so much else in theatre, what you see and hear when you experience the finished product is only a tiny part of what has gone on behind the scenes.

In professional theatre, actors, typically freelance, are usually paid for a three-, four- or five-week period of intense daily rehearsal before the opening of the show. That is a full-time commitment, although there may be the odd part of a day when a particular individual is not required because scenes he or she is involved in are not being worked on at that time.

Actors are expected to be in the building anything up to two hours before a show 'goes up' or starts. Costume and make-up has to be done and sometimes that is quite a complex, time-consuming process, depending on the show. A cast often warms up together before a show starts too.

Shows do not usually run on Sundays – a long tradition in theatre, although it is rapidly breaking down. If, however, a show is touring, the actors will often have to spend Sunday travelling to the next venue.

Actor Katharine Moraz, twenty-four, who graduated from Mountview Academy of Theatre Arts in 2010, toured in 2011 and 2012 with the highly successful *Avenue Q*, in which she played Kate Monster.

The show went all over the country, usually for a week in each venue – Brighton, Liverpool, Newcastle, Southend, Canterbury, Nottingham and many more. Moraz and her colleagues spent most Sundays moving on in readiness for Monday's technical rehearsal in the new venue. A schedule like this is pretty relentless.

Actors are usually contractually required to help publicise the show they're in as and when asked to do so by the company's or venue's marketing and publicity staff. Throughout the *Avenue Q* tour, for instance, Moraz and her colleagues did interviews with local TV and radio stations, as well as newspapers and magazines, almost everywhere they went. It is yet another commitment and call on the actor's time.

Many shows tour one- and two-night stands rather than whole weeks. Derby-based Oddsocks, for example, tours a five-actor, open-air Shakespeare each summer, and a winter family show – doing several shows a week all over the country from Newcastle to the Channel Islands.

Oddsocks mostly uses a minibus for the people and a mid-size van for the set. They take it in turns to drive so a clean driving licence is another near-essential for an actor – as is plenty of stamina for travelling and unloading because in companies such as this, actors usually have to double as stage managers too.

Ideally, while an actor is in a show – the contract for which will have a fixed time limit – he or she is auditioning for, or maybe even rehearsing for, the next job elsewhere. That will mean time spent reading, preparing and learning lines.

Although the repertory system has largely disappeared – to the sorrow of many older actors for whom it was a fine training – some venues still manage to operate within it. Queen's Theatre Hornchurch, for example, maintains an employed ensemble of actors who perform whatever the company produces, sometimes with extra actors brought in on a freelance basis.

That means that these actors perform a show in the evenings, at the same time as rehearsing the next show, and probably reading and working on the one after that. It is a full-time job requiring high-level 'multitasking' skills.

Another area of actors' work is theatre for young audiences, a sector which has grown enormously in recent years. London has theatres, such as Polka in Wimbledon, the Unicorn at London Bridge and Half Moon Young People's Theatre in Limehouse, entirely devoted to work for children and young people. And there are dozens of touring companies presenting work – from exquisite shows for children under three to gritty realism for those over fourteen – all over the country.

Actors working in young people's theatre have, arguably, an even harder job than their colleagues in West End musicals or well-established touring shows for adults. If a young child is bored, he or she won't usually be polite. There will be fidgeting and chatter, or in the case of the very youngest, crying or crawling away – and once teenagers start texting you've probably lost them. 'Children are the finest and most exacting critics. We have to entertain and engage them without ever patronising them – which is never easy,' veteran children's playwright and producer David Wood told me.

All the actors discussed so far are, of course, the lucky ones – who are in work. As everyone knows, even for talented actors there are too few jobs to go round, and nearly all actors have to cope with long periods of unemployment, euphemistically known as 'resting'.

No one has accurate figures, but it is thought that at any time over three quarters of Britain's trained, professional actors are resting. There is also a high drop-out rate in the early years as young actors simply give up and retrain for a job which will pay the bills reliably. That is why some experts argue that there are too many training places for actors and that it is wrong to be giving false expectations to so many young people for whom there will be little or no professional work.

But there are other ways in which a trained actor can deploy his or her professional talents between, or alongside, other jobs.

Work in education

There are several ways in which actors can double as educators.

Some companies, for example, specialise in taking work into schools.

Scene Productions creates work which is beginning to get bookings in venues patronised by the general public, but its core business is theatre-in-education and methodology relating to A level Theatre Studies.

Katharine Hurst, who runs the company with Kelly Taylor-Smith, offers an optional two-hour workshop for school students which guarantees a very informed and engaged audience for a show highlighting the techniques of Brecht, Artaud and Berkoff. It's an entertaining demonstration of how these ideas can be used to create dynamic physical theatre using grotesque masks, bold accurate gestures, screens, minimal 'representative' scenery, or realism and much more.

After the performance, the three actors run a short Q&A session to consolidate the learning still further before – often – dashing off in their minibus to another school.

It is intensive and worthwhile work for the actors that Hurst and Taylor-Smith employ.

Be a part-time supply teacher

Bigfoot started out in 2000 as a very small drama-workshop company working in a few schools. Today Bigfoot Arts Education is one of the UK's largest independent arts-education companies, providing creative-arts-based learning.

Its specially trained 'Bigfooters' – usually actors who use drama, visual art, dance and music – run creative workshops and courses helping over fifteen thousand pupils a week to discover their spark in early-years-, primary- and secondary-learning environments.

One of Bigfoot's most innovative schemes (and it has many) is its specialist agency. It offers a planned absence-cover service for schools. Effectively it means that actors cover for teachers. The aim is to change the way in which drama and the performing arts are used to help support and enrich curriculum topics, and to offer children access to high-quality creative learning experiences. The service offers creative workshops through specially designed lesson plans tailored to the classroom and school hall, and are used to cover teachers' planned absences, sickness cover and so on.

It's a good way for actors to do valuable work which exploits their own skills – and also helps pay their bills.

Facilitate for company education departments

A large education department will employ – on a freelance basis, but it's often quite frequent and regular – teams of people trained to lead show-related and other workshops for school students.

Sometimes these take place in the theatre – perhaps in the morning before a matinee performance. In other cases, the team goes to the school and leads the work there. Such workshops may be led by the actors the students will also see in the performance, or by other facilitators. Some of these leaders will be former teachers but many will be actors.

The RSC offers its thirty-month ensemble actors at Stratford an opportunity to undertake postgraduate training in the teaching of Shakespeare. It equips them to work for the RSC as facilitators during the time they work for the company, and provides them with another marketable skill. RSC's actors also lead training courses for teachers wanting to learn how to teach Shakespeare better and more interactively.

Actors working in schools in any capacity must, of course, be fully checked by the DBS so that they can show that they are fit to work with young people or vulnerable adults.

Teach performing-arts skills to children in a part-time school

Many professional performers have decided, for example, that taking a franchise with a stage-school chain such Helen O'Grady Drama Academy, Razzamataz Theatre School or LIPA 4:19 Part Time Academy is a useful part-time supplement to income. Or, if you don't want the responsibility of that, you can apply for a teaching post within one. Classes often run on Saturday mornings so can usually be slotted in alongside auditions, rehearsals or performances, if an actor is lucky enough to be in work.

Stagecoach Theatre Arts, for example, is by far the biggest player in the field. Based in Surrey, it now has over six hundred schools in the UK reaching over thirty thousand children, and another hundred or so overseas.

Denise Hutton-Gosney, founder of Razzamataz with over thirty-five franchises from Ayr to Torquay and from Whitehaven to Maidstone, says: 'Our Carlisle office has enquiries every week from potential franchisees.' Hutton-Gosney's company has benefited from good TV publicity, including support from Duncan Bannatyne, and she keeps her prices at competitive levels. 'We also have seventy teachers working in Thomson/ First Choice holiday resorts and many families book holidays specifically so that the children can have the Razzamataz experience,' she says.

Founded in Australia, Helen O'Grady Drama Academy is doing well too, with new schools continuing to open. Its franchises in Britain, based mostly in schools and village halls, reach fifteen thousand children per week. Now run globally from the Channel Islands, it also operates in twenty-two other countries and reaches a total of fifty thousand children per week worldwide. Other ways in which Helen O'Grady is building its business is by diversifying and offering more 'add-ons', such as pre-school classes which it calls 'Kindy drama'. First piloted in four schools, these sessions are gradually being made more widely available. And, in 2011, Nigel Le Page, owner of the business, and his colleagues began to offer adult classes in some areas. 'We are expanding our after-schools-clubs business too as headteachers realise the value of buying in a product like ours,' he says.

Beyond the many franchised schools, there are hundreds of independent stand-alone schools across the UK teaching children performing-arts skills, on a part-time basis.

And it all makes supplementary, relevant work for actors.

Work as a corporate actor

These days, many actors generate a substantial part of their income by doing corporate role-play and training, using the skills they acquired at drama school in a workplace situation.

Commercial companies want training videos, people to train their staff in presentation skills, and experts in 'getting the show on the road' to run their events.

Actors are needed for all of this, although it rarely features in drama-school training programmes.

Alongside film and television work, Paul Clayton has been involved in the corporate sector since 1993. He has directed over three hundred live events for production companies and large-scale corporate clients, and does one-to-one presentation training for senior executives at many companies, such as McDonald's UK. He has also worked as a corporate casting director (and still does) for many production companies, finding them actors for various different events, videos, and conference sessions.

Clayton has run role-play training sessions for actors at the Actors Centre, of which he is now co-chairman. On a freelance basis, he has worked as a roleplayer for eighteen years with clients in both the public and private sectors at all levels of engagement.

'A successful corporate actor can easily earn £2,000 or more a month from role-play work. It enables them then to go off and do low-paid theatre jobs and feed their souls, or to hang around for the right television job but still feed their families.'

Form a company of your own

Work tends not to come looking for newly trained young actors although, of course, some are lucky.

Rather than resting passively, actors are increasingly forming small companies, creating their own work and taking it out on the road, as Filskit Theatre does. The annual Edinburgh Festival Fringe has hundreds, if not thousands of such companies performing every year. There are several pub-theatres in London and elsewhere offering small, affordable playing spaces.

Some drama schools now actively train their students to think proactively about creating work when they leave.

FORM A COMPANY OF YOUR OWN

> The New Diorama Theatre, a small venue near Euston
> Station, helps new small companies to create work by,
> for example, offering affordable space and time for
> research and development.
>
> New Diorama Theatre is unique in London by its ded-
> ication to presenting the work of theatre companies
> – emerging and established – within a variety of gen-
> res, everything from straight theatre to comedy and
> opera are welcome.
>
> They want to find and support the next generation of
> Complicites, Kneehighs or Headlongs while also offer-
> ing a space to established companies wanting to work
> in intimate spaces.
>
> By sourcing great theatre companies making quality
> work from festivals, other theatres and abroad, NDT
> ensure that they are presenting the very best groups
> and supporting them in their development.
>
> *Adapted from New Diorama Theatre website*

It is a matter of being entrepreneurial and learning from
your experience. It is better for any actor to be performing
– even to the smallest of audiences – than it is to be 'temp-
ing' and wondering whether to give up and become a police
officer or a retail manager.

If you are on stage, you are building your CV, and there's
always a chance of your being spotted by an agent, director
or theatre director. I have often seen such people quietly sitting in the audience at fringe shows. Don't underestimate it
as a way of getting noticed.

And remember – the well-known companies almost always
started from very small beginnings.

How do you become an actor?

You have to train – long and hard. And sensible, successful actors never stop training.

Do not be fooled by TV talent-spotting shows, which imply that if you have innate raw talent you can just walk in off the street and strut your stuff successfully on the stages of the West End.

Training teaches you how to develop and apply your talent. It also ensures that you build up your stamina. A successful stage performer needs as much energy as an athlete – and you wouldn't expect to play for Manchester United without years of ongoing training to build your skills and strength.

Seasoned actors make it look effortless. It isn't. Far from it. Making it look easy is part of what actors are trained to do. Acting is, after all, entirely about creating convincing illusions.

It is sometimes argued that the three lead children in the Harry Potter Films – Daniel Radcliffe, Emma Watson and Rupert Grint – have all made very successful careers without training.

They have not. Although they didn't go to a drama school or other performing-arts vocational-course provider, they were very carefully trained for ten years through working on the seven films. They were given intensive skills training, including voice and movement.

It would be truer to say that these three trained for far longer than most actors, who spend just three years in drama school, college or university.

There are a number of ways of training…

Drama school

Drama UK (formed in 2012 from a merger of the old National Council for Drama Training, NCDT, and Conference of Drama Schools, CDS) is the linking body for the UK's key drama schools.

These include RADA, LAMDA, Bristol Old Vic Theatre School, Liverpool Institute of Performing Arts (LIPA), Royal Conservatoire of Scotland and others. Most are fairly well known and you will find them listed with further details and links on Drama UK's website, and in the appendix of this book.

Some of these schools have been absorbed by universities in which they are now, effectively, a department. For example, Birmingham School of Acting is part of Birmingham City University, East 15 is part of University of Essex, and Guildford School of Acting (GSA) is part of the University of Surrey. Manchester School of Theatre has always been part of Manchester Metropolitan University.

They still function as vocational drama schools, however, with considerable autonomy vested in the principal and his or her staff. The advantage of 'belonging' to a university is that the drama school has access to its funding – which directly benefits the students.

The University of Essex, for instance, has invested heavily in excellent premises for East 15's satellite campus at Southend, and in new buildings at Loughton. And GSA, which used to be in quaint but inadequate buildings in the town centre, is now in a state-of-the-art new building on the University of Surrey's nearby Stag Hill Campus.

Most of the two- and three-year undergraduate courses in the main twenty-two Drama UK schools are degree or foundation-degree courses.

Although no one in the industry will be much interested in the pieces of paper you've been awarded to demonstrate your skills (a degree-holder's pirouette or convincing solil-oquy is much like any other – either you can do it or you can't), if you're on a course which is labelled 'degree' and accredited by a university, you are entitled to exactly the same loans and funding as for any other degree.

A course accredited by Drama UK in one of its core schools should offer you thirty hours a week of tuition. That usually includes voice, movement, dance, combat, singing and many other aspects of acting that a well-trained actor needs. Drama students also rehearse and present a number of shows during the course and often take part in community projects and other activities built into the course. At the same time, they are expected to be reading and researching the work they are engaged in – a play set in a historical period, perhaps – and often learning lines.

Students usually arrive in the building for a 9.00 a.m. start and are often still at work well into the evening, especially if there's a show coming up – when there could be weekend rehearsals as well.

Drama students work very hard indeed and often express surprise at how little their friends on other university courses seem to be required to do in comparison.

'I knew nothing about drama school and neither did anyone else at my Kent grammar school, but Mountview was on the UCAS form and I had actually heard of it so, rather hesitantly, I put it down as my last choice after university. I loved the audition and, amazingly, was offered a place.

The training was absolutely great. Hard work but brilliant. And my parents were very supportive in helping me to pay for it.

I was signed by an agent following the graduation showcase, after which I did some work for children at Greenwich Theatre, followed by *The Laramie Project*, a play also at Greenwich. *Winnie the Witch* in Manchester was a good learning experience because I had to learn puppetry, which I used again when I toured with *Avenue Q*. I was Gretel in Theatre Royal Margate's Christmas show *Hansel and Gretel* too.

Training is essential. The level of commitment makes you sure it's what you really want to do. It breaks you down and then builds you up again so that you're fit for anything – and it taught me the philosophy that you never stop learning. I certainly wouldn't have got anywhere without it.

And it really is true that training is a lifelong process. For example, I played piano and saxophone at school but knew I'd never be good enough to be a performing musician. However, I can work as an actor-musician. I've taught myself guitar and ukulele and had to play an accordion in *Hansel and Gretel*. I'm only happy if I'm learning something new.'

Katharine Moraz

Stuart Walker, twenty-three, graduated from East 15's BA in Acting in 2011. He got interested in acting through doing the graded speech and drama exams set by LAMDA for school students.

He saw *Death of a Salesman* and Alan Bennett's *The History Boys* and came out both times convinced that it was something he could do too. Then he did a one-week summer school at East 15. 'It was completely different from anything I'd ever done before. I discovered that there were such things as voice classes and movement lessons. I made up my mind there and then that I never wanted to do academic study again, and I applied for the full-time course.'

Soon after graduation, Walker played Gregor in Scene Productions' version of *Metamorphosis* and was in their show *Vampirates* which toured to schools and other venues, often with workshops, for many months. He was also in a Radio 3 play and had some work performed at the Old Red Lion soon after leaving East 15. He did two months street theatre in London, Madrid and Lisbon too.

'Training is vital,' he says. 'It gives you the experience so that you don't panic when things go wrong. Two or three years at drama school teaches you to handle almost anything.'

Training philosophies

There have been many great theatre practitioners whose ideas, theories and methods have informed drama teaching in the last hundred years or so – from Russia, USA, Britain and the rest of Europe. This is certainly not an exhaustive list or in any particular order, but they include:

- Konstantin Stanislavsky

- Antonin Artaud

- Jerzy Grotowski

- Stella Adler

- Lee Strasberg

- Bertolt Brecht

- Michael Chekhov

- Peter Brook

- Steven Berkoff

Drama students will be familiar with these names and be able to use some of the techniques they advocate(d).

Some courses in some schools and colleges aim to offer students a mixed palette so that each individual can gradually work out for him or herself, with guidance, what works best. Other training courses are fairly closely attuned to a particular way of working.

Any student thinking of applying for a course should ask about the training philosophy of the college and whether it is eclectic or prescriptive.

Different sorts of drama courses

Some courses are simply labelled 'acting', although some singing and dancing will always feature because good, accomplished acting so often includes them.

Almost all drama schools now offer degrees or other qualifications in musical theatre.

And there are other options. Some colleges, as we've seen, offer courses in actor-musicianship. If you play instruments but are not up to concert standard – or don't want to pursue a career in music – but want to perform, it could be worth considering this training option. More and more 'straight' (that is, not musical theatre) shows, especially for young audiences, seem to include actors making live music.

Don't forget courses focusing on education or community work either – such as the one Blair Underwoode (see page 172) is doing at Royal Central School of Speech and Drama – or the Community and Applied Theatre one at Birmingham School of Acting.

Postgraduate courses

Would a one-year course leading to an MA or a postgraduate certificate give you the training you need, if you've already done a degree? Possibly. Postgraduate students are a very disparate group.

Some are students who opt to do a more academic, non-vocational degree first in, say, law or physics, perhaps pressurised by parents worried about employment prospects in the performing-arts industries. Some of these then decide to spend just one more year having a serious go at what they wanted to do in the first place before deciding whether to enrol on, say, a retail-management course with Marks and Spencer – or to start auditioning for professional roles in theatre, TV or film, or looking for backstage opportunities.

Then there are those who have just completed a first degree in drama or a related discipline and immediately want to take their studies to a higher level before they begin work. That can mean staying on in the same institution to complete what, effectively, becomes a four-year training course, although many students choose to move to another school or college for their postgraduate work.

It can be a way of studying a specific angle very closely. Theatre for young audiences, for example, is a big growth area and Rose Bruford offers a very practical MA for actors who want to specialise in it.

Other students take a postgraduate course in pursuit of something more practical and skills-based than the original degree, especially if it was taught in a university rather than a specialist drama school – a problem we will look at in a little more detail shortly. The latter option often means transferring to a different training institution.

Another group is working actors – and other performing-arts practitioners – for whom a postgraduate degree, studied full or part time, is top-up training or continuing professional development. For some of these people, it can lead to work in related professions such as dramaturgy, facilitation, therapeutic drama, teaching and so on.

There are always postgraduate students who have long since qualified and worked for some years in a completely different field such as retail, health, finance or local government. Now, perhaps, armed with a redundancy package, they are looking for a change of direction.

The major problem with postgraduate degrees is that there is no public funding for them so you have to pay your own fees (see later in this chapter for information about funding).

Many students work, not necessarily in theatre, for a while after their first degree in order to save up for the MA – if that is what they think they need or want.

Drama training in a university

Many – if not most – universities offer courses in drama.

Teachers and parents sometimes see these as the ideal way forward because they think that the student gets the benefit and kudos of a university education, which is perceived as 'safer' than a drama school.

This is a misconception. It is important to understand that few university drama departments (although there are some notable exceptions, such as the very practical and useful course at University of Kent) are offering viable vocational training.

Students usually get a fraction of the teaching hours they would have the benefit of in a drama school, and there is likely to be more theory and less practical work. This could be an excellent grounding for a career as a playwright, theatre administrator or arts journalist, but it could well be inadequate for a budding actor.

It is very important to be clear what you want from your course. If you want practical, vocational training, make sure you are in an institution that can give you the day-in, day-out, intensive teaching and support that you need. Be sure that the tuition is coming from people with real recent industry experience rather than from theorists.

I meet many students in vocational training who tell me that they went to university first but still felt at the end of the course that they were untrained, so they have now enrolled somewhere else. That means more training to fund and it's much harder for a second degree.

Some students are very bitter about the 'mistake' they made in going to university in the first place. Many feel cheated and misled – which is probably unreasonable. Universities are pretty clear about what they're offering on the whole.

If you are considering a university drama course:

- Read the small print in the prospectus.

- Attend an open day and ask questions.

- Find out how many hours of voice, movement, acting and other classes are programmed each week.

- Where are the course alumni working now?

- Who are the tutors and what is their industry experience?

- Make enquiries about the number of shows students work on each year.

- Talk to students already on the course about their experiences and seek their views.

You shouldn't feel embarrassed about probing. The university wants to sell you its 'product'. You are the customer. And nobody wants you to make a costly, time-wasting mistake by choosing the wrong sort of course.

Some students do deliberately plan university first. When I caught up with twenty-two-year-old student Alex Hammond, he was just out of a long rehearsal of the musical, *The Pajama Game*, his head and notebook full of detailed notes from director Karen Rabinowitz. He was playing Sid, the lead role, and it was one week to the opening night.

Hammond was approaching the end of the one-year, highly intensive, postgraduate music-theatre diploma course at the Royal Academy of Music (RAM), of which Rabinowitz is course leader. 'I did a three-year BA in Theatre and Performance at Leeds University because I wanted a secure academic background first. But I'd had ten years of amateur experience. Before that I was always determined to come here to the Royal Academy of Music after university.'

He added: 'I'd heard about this course and it has been everything I'd hoped. Everyone on staff at the RAM is at the top of their game and they really make sure you understand the craft.'

Other courses

We've talked a lot about Drama UK's core schools in this section and elsewhere in the book. But there are, of course, other options.

Many independent – that is, not part of the state-funded further- or higher-education system – schools are offering good training too. But there are two caveats.

First, because these schools are essentially private establishments, students mostly have to pay their own fees, although there may be scholarships and bursaries.

Second, some of them are excellent and some are *not*. This is a cut-throat business and there are schools out there who are simply after your money in return for very poor training which won't equip you for anything much. So do your research thoroughly.

Drama UK has three levels of endorsement. At the top are its accredited schools. Below that are other schools it inspects and approves. The final tier is schools that simply opt to be listed on Drama UK's website.

Any school that has Drama UK approval comes with a certain level of quality assurance, so begin your research by checking the Drama UK website.

Then start asking questions, some of which will be answered on each school's website. Use this as a checklist:

- Is the school oversubscribed, and if so by how much? (Major drama schools often get fifty or more applications for every place because they have such a fine reputation.)

- How many hours of tuition will you get per week? (You need at least thirty.)

- Who are the tutors and what are their industry credentials? (They should be experienced, ideally current, industry practitioners as well as good teachers.)

- How large are class sizes? (Twenty is plenty and smaller is better. Thirty is too many.)

- How many leavers are signed by well-established, respected agents at the end of the course? (If the course is up to scratch, many of the students will have agents when they leave.)

- Where are people who have done this course in the past now working? (If the course is good, many of them will be getting paid professional jobs and building their experience and profiles.)

And if you are invited to audition, listen to your instincts. A good school will:

- Give you plenty of time. The best auditions last a whole day for everyone. The worst begin to eliminate and dismiss rejected applicants after a very short time.
- Take the trouble to make you feel comfortable.
- Give you the chance to show what you can do in a range of situations, such as group work.
- Introduce you to current students and encourage you to chat to them.
- Provide you with feedback whichever way your audition goes.
- Make sure you get value for money from your day (there is almost always a charge for a drama school audition).

Founded in 2009 by Annemarie Lewis Thomas with just twelve students, Musical Theatre Academy is based in its own studios in London's Holloway Road. It now has almost its full complement of forty students. It offers an intensive, full-time, two-year course in musical theatre, and has places for twenty students in each year. Almost all its students are signed by agents at the end of the course and impressive numbers of them have pleasing volumes of work. The emphasis is on 'ethical training', and Principal Lewis Thomas works very hard to keep costs down and to plough any surplus back into the college to benefit the students. All the tutors are current West End professionals. MTA won *The Stage* 100 Awards School of the Year in 2012.

Samantha Hull, twenty-two, completed MTA's two-year course in 2011. A ballet buff from babyhood, she had always attended classes part-time.

Straight into employment after college, Hull was one of the thirteen performers in Impact Opera's *Carmen* at Yvonne Arnaud Theatre, Guildford. 'It was wonderful experience to work with opera singers!' she says. Then it was off to Tel Aviv for a two-week run of *A Chorus Line* with Bronowski Productions. She was Fairy of the Rings in Theatre Royal Wakefield's *Aladdin* over Christmas then, early in 2012, came a production of *Don Giovanni*, in which she danced, took non-singing roles and acted as movement director. This was followed by a national tour in *Angelina Ballerina*.

'Well, of course, the big dream is the West End,' she says. 'But for the moment I'm just delighted to have so much work immediately after completing training.'

Training part-time

If you want to train as a professional performer, is part-time training really a viable option?

Students who work, for example, with Daniel Brennan at Actor Works, with Giles Foreman at the Giles Foreman Centre for Acting, those who've signed up for one of Brian Timoney's boot camps, or at a GSA Saturday School are convinced it is.

The truth is that it may make good sense for some aspirant performing-arts professionals to train part time. The cost of training to study drama full time is frighteningly high – even for those students on courses accredited by Drama UK. The prospect of incurring massive debts, understandably, deters some students and their families.

The Actor Works, based in Wapping, was founded by Daniel Brennan in 2007 and runs several different courses. There's a part-time evening course (twice a week) for those who want to study acting as a leisure activity. A part-time foundation course is taught three days a week for fifteen weeks and prepares students for entry to drama school. Then there's a vocational course for all ages running evenings and weekends. Although the Actor Works uses a variety of methods and approaches, it is the work of Viola Spolin — not very well known in the UK — which is the strongest influence on the school's ethos.

But you will need stamina and a lot of dedication. The evening and weekend course requires students to attend every weekday evening from 6.30 p.m. to 10.30 p.m., all day Saturday and occasional Sundays – which adds up to at least a twenty-six-hour commitment each week on top of the day job.

So what are the part-time options? Part-time training can mean attending on one, or often several, evenings per week. Sometimes the training runs at weekends, or both. Summer schools or short courses are another way of doing it. If it's good-quality, serious training, it will be fairly intensive.

The big plus, of course, for adults is that the day job pays the bills, including the cost of training, so you can, with care, avoid the worst of all that disheartening debt. Part-time training also allows you to hedge your bets by keeping another line of work going in case drama training doesn't lead quite where you'd like it to.

The Brian Timoney Actors' Studio, in North London, teaches Method Acting mostly through three-day courses known as 'boot camps'. It expanded its operation in autumn 2009 to offer a one-year, part-time course in Method Acting using the techniques of practitioners such as Lee Strasberg. It involves twelve 3-day weekends per year and includes a Method Acting 'boot camp' in Los Angeles. This year, the Brian Timoney Actors' Studio ran its first Young Actors' Boot Camp.

Some people argue that actors and other performers, if they are going to be good, need plenty of broadening experience of 'real life' – which they won't find while immured in a full-time drama school with other trainee actors. Part-time trainees get this from the back-up job.

There's a newish foundation course in dance with musical theatre in Cornwall. Jason Thomas Performing Arts has been teaching children and adults across the county for some time, but the acquisition of premises in Truro means it can now also offer a foundation course – Cornwall's first. Mindful of the difficulties of funding full-time training, Thomas and his colleagues are running their course from Monday to Thursday (9.15 a.m. to 4.00 p.m.) for three 12-week terms, so that students have enough space left in the week to be able to work part-time alongside their studies if they need to.

Foundation courses

You can apply to train as an actor straight from school at age eighteen as Katharine Moraz and Stuart Walker did. Or, as many students choose to do, you can enrol on a self-funded one-year foundation course first to help you with audition technique and the building-up of performance skills.

Some major drama schools run foundation courses, at the end of which some students successfully apply for the full degree course in the same school. Others apply successfully to train elsewhere. Some inevitably aren't up to standard and don't get in anywhere, although determined students sometimes apply several times over two or three years – maintaining skills levels throughout – and eventually get a place. And there are always some who decide at the end of a foundation course that a performance career isn't what they want after all, so they go off and train for something else.

LAMDA and Oxford School of Drama are just two of Drama UK's main schools to offer foundation courses – there are others. Arts Educational Schools London runs a part-time one.

Independent colleges offering foundation courses – with a good record for getting students into schools running accredited courses at the end of the year – include Preparation Performance Academy (PPA) in Guildford and Read College in Reading.

Blair Underwoode chose the part-time foundation course (three days a week from 9.30 a.m. to 5.30 p.m.) at Dorset School of Acting, based at Poole and completed in summer 2011.

She then went on to full-time training at Royal Central School of Speech and Drama to do its BA (Hons) in Drama, Applied Theatre and Education. Her long-term plan is to be employed in community and education work.

'The DSA programme is very good,' she says, 'especially the toolkit, based on Stanislavsky, which has been invaluable. We were taught singing. We also had voice classes, dance classes, sessions for readings and so on. The masterclasses with Mel Churcher were excellent too.'

DSA was founded in 2010. Every student in its first intake gained a full-time place in one of Drama UK's schools.

Funding your training

Anything I say about funding is liable to be out of date before you read this. The situation and the rules change all the time. You should always ask the school/college/university or other training provider which is offering you a place for up-to-date advice.

What follows is a brief summary of the funding situation at the time of writing along, with a few ideas about how to help yourself.

Performing-arts courses leading to accredited, undergraduate degrees, including two-year foundation degrees, in specialist colleges or universities can be funded with student loans like any other degree. These have to be paid back eventually, but not until (or unless) your earnings reach £21,000 per year and, failing that, the debt is written off after thirty years. The Student Loans Company can provide details about exactly how these loans work.

Grants – which do not have to be repaid – are available from the government for students from very low-income backgrounds to help cover the cost of both tuition fees and living expenses.

Dance and Drama Awards (DaDAs) are government-funded scholarships. Top performing-arts training colleges are assigned a handful of these to offer to outstanding students. These are due to be phased out, but the government promised early in 2012 that it would maintain them until a new, replacement system is developed.

There is no public funding for foundation courses, which typically last one year and help students to prepare for drama school. Neither is there any government help available for postgraduate study. It's worth noting that, even for a post-graduate degree, you can access the normal loans and grants system only once. If you have already been funded to do a degree in, say, physics or law, you are ineligible for loans and grants for a subsequent performing-arts degree.

If you do any sort of training in an independent college or school which is outside the accredited system, you cannot access public funds and must pay your own fees and accommodation costs.

Career-development loans can sometimes be used to fund training, particularly at postgraduate level. Barclays and The Co-operative Bank are best for these.

Many training providers offer – or have benefactors who do – some scholarship places on courses of all sorts. *The Stage* promotes over £600,000 worth of these every year. Talk to the schools you're interested in applying to about scholar-ship availability and the application process.

Otherwise it's a case of looking for ways of raising money to fund yourself. That means making money and saving money.

Try the entrepreneurial route. You are, presumably, a talented person if you want to train in the performing arts. Why not give a concert? Sell raffle tickets and get your family to make cakes to sell. Think of it as good old-fashioned fundraising. I have talked to several students who've done this very successfully.

Seek sponsorship. Try writing to a lot of people very persuasively and asking for a small amount, such as £10.00. Again, a number of students have told me that they've worked very hard at this and managed to accrue useful sums towards their training.

Read Lyndi Smith's book *Free Degrees*. She funded herself most of the way through RADA without incurring any debt at all and she has some good ideas.

Consult the *Directory of Grant Making Trusts* in your local library or online. Hundreds of organisations have money to give to the right people. Some of the organisations listed help only specific groups, such as the residents of inner London boroughs or the children of the clergy. Make sure your criteria fit the category the organisations are set up to help and apply to all the relevant ones.

An ALRA (Academy of Live and Dramatic Art) student told me about Share and Care UK (www.shareandcare.co.uk). It's an agency which places people needing low-cost accommodation in the homes of people with care needs who are prepared to let a room in return for ten hours a week of housework, gardening, cooking and so on. Juliet Chappell reckons she saved about £4,000 in her first year and made firm friends with the elderly lady she stayed with.

Don't spend money unnecessarily either. If you are serious about your training, this could be a good moment to reconsider your relationship with tobacco and alcohol, both very costly. Accept that you won't be able to afford many clothes while you're training and study the rudiments of good housekeeping to keep living expenses down. Buy ingredients and cook them rather then relying on takeaways, and plan meals in advance with housemates, for example.

Further reading

The Acting Book, John Abbott (Nick Hern Books, 2012)

Behind the Curtain: The Job of Acting, Peter Bowles (Oberon Books, 2012)

Directory of Grant Making Trusts, Directory of Social Change (new edition every two years)

Free Degrees, Lyndi Smith (White Lion Press, 2009)

In-depth Acting, Dee Cannon (Oberon Books, 2012)

The Methuen Drama Dictionary of the Theatre, ed. Jonathan Law (Methuen Drama, 2012)

The Monologue Audition: A Practical Guide for Actors, Karen Kohlhass (Nick Hern Books, 2009)

Oily Cart: All Sorts of Theatre for All Sorts of Kids, Mark Brown (Trentham, 2012)

So You Want to Be A Corporate Actor?, Paul Clayton (Nick Hern Books, 2013)

Thank You That's All We Need for Today… A Practical Guide to Music Theatre Auditions, Mary Hammond (Edition Peters, 2009)

Useful websites

The Actor Works www.actorworks.org

Bigfoot www.bigfoot-theatre.co.uk

The Brian Timoney Actors' Studio
www.briantimoneyacting.co.uk

Directory of Grant Making Trusts
www.dsc.org.uk/Publications/Fundraisingsources/@132337

Drama UK www.dramauk.co.uk

Edinburgh Festival Fringe www.edfringe.com

Jason Thomas Performing Arts
www.jasonthomasdance.co.uk

Musical Theatre Academy www.themta.co.uk

New Diorama Theatre www.newdiorama.com

PPA www.ppacademy.co.uk

Read College www.rdtc.org.uk

Scene Productions www.sceneproductions.co.uk

Student Loans Company www.slc.co.uk

And Lastly...

If you want to work in theatre in any capacity, you need flair, determination, talent and, in most cases, top-quality training – as we've seen.

You also need something else which can't be learned, earned, bought, measured or planned for. And nearly everyone I've spoken to in connection with this book has mentioned it.

You need *luck*. And you need it in spadesful. I wish you plenty of it.

Training in the UK

These members of Drama UK are schools which run some accredited courses. Although most began as independent colleges many, but not all, now operate as part of a university.

All teach acting. In most cases they also run a range of courses at various levels in other aspects of performance, such as musical theatre. Many of these schools run a good range of backstage course too.

Students are usually entitled to the normal student loans and other funding for foundation degrees and full degree courses in these schools.

Academy of Live and Dramatic Arts (ALRA)
Studio 24, Royal Victoria Patriotic Building, John Archer Way, London SW18 3SX
020 8870 6475, www.alra.co.uk

Arts Educational Schools (ArtsEd)
Cone Ripman House, 14 Bath Road, Chiswick, London W4 1LY
020 8987 6666, www.artsed.co.uk

Birmingham School of Acting (BSA)
Millennium Point, Curzon Street, Birmingham B4 7XG
0121 331 7220, www.bcu.ac.uk/pme/school-of-acting

Bristol Old Vic Theatre School
1–2 Downside Road, Clifton, Bristol BS8 2XF
0117 973 3535, www.oldvic.ac.uk

Drama Centre London
Granary Building, 1 Granary Square, King's Cross,
London, N1C 4AA
020 7514 7444, www.csm.arts.ac.uk/dramacentrelondon

Drama Studio London
Grange Court, 1 Grange Road, Ealing W5 5QN
020 8579 3897, www.dramastudiolondon.co.uk

East 15 Acting School
Hatfields, Rectory Lane, Loughton IG10 3RY
020 8508 5983, www.east15.ac.uk

Guildford School of Acting (GSA)
Stag Hill Campus, Guildford, Surrey GU2 7XH
01483 684040, www.gsauk.org

Guildhall School of Music and Drama (GSMD)
Barbican, Silk Street, London EC2Y 8DT
020 7628 2571, www.gsmd.ac.uk

Italia Conti School of Theatre Arts
Avondale, 72 Landor Road, London SW9 9PH
020 7733 3210, www.italiaconti.com

Liverpool Institute of Performing Arts (LIPA)
Mount Street, Liverpool L1 9HF
0151 330 3000, www.lipa.ac.uk

London Academy of Music and Dramatic Art (LAMDA)
155 Talgarth Road, London W14 9DA
020 8834 0500, www.lamda.org.uk

Manchester Metropolitan University School of Theatre
(MMU)
Mabel Tylecote Building, Cavendish Street, Manchester,
M15 6BG
0161 247 1751, www.theatre.mmu.ac.uk

Mountview Academy of Theatre Arts
Clarendon Road, London N22 6XF
020 8881 2201, www.mountview.org.uk

Oxford School of Drama
Sansomes Farm Studios, Woodstock, Oxfordshire
OX20 1ER
01993 812883, www.oxforddrama.ac.uk

Rose Bruford College
Lamorbey Park, Burnt Oak Lane, Sidcup, Kent DA15 9DF
020 8308 2600, www.bruford.ac.uk

Royal Academy of Dramatic Art (RADA)
62–64 Gower Street, London WC1E 6ED
020 7636 7076, www.rada.ac.uk

Royal Central School of Speech And Drama (CSSD)
Eton Avenue, London NW3 3HY
020 7722 8183, www.cssd.ac.uk

Royal Conservatoire of Scotland
100 Renfrew Street, Glasgow G2 3DB
0141 332 4101, www.rcs.ac.uk

Royal Welsh College of Music and Drama
Castle Grounds, Cathays Park, Cardiff CF1 3ER
02920 342854, www.rwcmd.ac.uk

Please note that although this list was correct at time of publication, schools may change their accreditation status.

Some chains of part-time class providers

The Courage to Sing
16 Duke's Way, Axminster, Devon EX13 5QP
01297 639922, www.thecouragetosing.co.uk

Debutots Ltd
Suite 143, 179 Whiteladies Road, Bristol BS8 2AG
0845 519 4941, www.debutots.co.uk

Helen O'Grady Drama Academy CI Ltd
North Side, Vale, Guernsey GY3 5TX
01481 200250, www.helenogrady.co.uk

LIPA 4:19
Liverpoool Institue for Performing Arts, Mount Street,
Liverpool L1 9HF
0151 330 3009,
www.lipa.ac.uk/content/LIPA419Franchise.aspx

Music Bugs
4 Bowles Road, Swindon, Wiltshire SN25 4ZN
0844 578 1010, www.musicbugs.co.uk

The Pauline Quirke Academy of Performing Arts
Custodia House, Queensmead Road, Loudwater, High
Wycombe, Buckinghamshire HP10 9XA
0845 673 2022, www.pqacademy.com

Razzamataz Theatre Schools
Atlas Works, Nelson Street, Carlisle CA2 5NB
01228 550129, www.razzamataz.co.uk

Soundsteps
11 Ashcroft Rise, Coulsdon, Surrey CR5 2SS
020 8668 4825, www.soundstepsmusic.co.uk

StageAbility Stage School
Vestry Hall, St Michael's Lane, Braintree, Essex CM7 1EY
01376 567677, www.stageability.co.uk

Stagecoach Theatre Arts Schools
The Courthouse, Elm Grove, Walton-on-Thames, Surrey
KT12 1LZ
01932 254333, www.stagecoach.co.uk

Theatretrain
121 Theydon Grove, Epping, Essex CM16 4QB
01327 300498, www.theatretrain.co.uk

www.nickhernbooks.co.uk

 facebook.com/nickhernbooks